2/ 12/ ∧ 9

THANK YO

CONTINUED SUPPORT !

Rob J Ry

MW00744958

gambling *for life*

SWINGING THE ODDS IN YOUR FAVOR
FOR MORE MONEY AND GREAT SEX

RJ REGAN

gambling for life

SWINGING THE ODDS IN YOUR FAVOR
FOR MORE MONEY AND GREAT SEX

preface

I almost always get a "you're kidding me, right?" response from people after reading the title; especially from those over forty and in the Christian community - until I explain what I mean.

For example, a majority of 17-25 year olds have two primary questions in their head - money and sex. If that is what they are interested in, I thought, "Why not talk about that and show them how."

In my research I uncovered the following:

Question: What do 90% of "Deca-millionaires" and 80% of millionaires have in common? (Other than just a lot of money)

Answer: They are all married to their first spouse.

Question: Who has the best sex in this country (as rated by quality as well as frequency)?

Answer: Married people

So, If you really are interested in money and sex, then it is in your best interest to get married and stay married. Now, what are you doing to become that man or woman worth marrying? The answer to that question is the basis for the book. I have put together the half dozen areas of life that I have found have the biggest impact on your life.

Now, because I am a follower of Christ and almost 80% of Americans say that they are Christians as well, this book has a Biblical wolrdview.

You may be thinking to yourself RJ, as a Christian, how does this teaching line up with not seeking after the things of the world but, rather seek after the things of Christ?" My response is one of priority and perspective.

My perspective is that all of our basic earthly and carnal desires have been given to us in creation. God made us a certain way. John Eldredge in his book *"Dare To Desire"* says that desire cannot be denied, it will be satisfied one way or another. The desire for money and sex are just the two of the most prevalent desires we have. He knows we have desires and needs, He made us with them. As such, He also gave us a way to have those desires filled, as prescribed by Him in the Bible.

Everything we have can be either used as a tool or an idol. Money and sex are no different. Money as an idol will harden your heart and build up a fortress of pride around you. However, money as a tool in the hands of a steward will soften your heart and lay to waste strongholds through wise investment in people and generosity in giving.

Sex as an idol will turn a man or women into a loaf of bread fit to be eaten by the birds in a desert wasteland. However, sex as a tool and properly used to protect ourselves from immorality and deception will destroy one of the enemy's most powerful strongholds on us.

The priority is that when these desires become a god unto themselves great evil is fostered. However, to deny these desires and pretend that they do not exist, or that they are in some way evil is one of the great deceptions of the enemy.

A favorite movie quote of mine is in the Usual Suspects. The character played by Kevin Spacy said, "The greatest lie the Devil ever told was to convince the world that he didn't exist."

Rest assured, there is a battle being waged. I did not chose to be in a battle, but a war wages on none the less. We are all being attacked with ideas, forces and temptations that lead to theft, destruction and death in our lives. Then there are the ideas that protect against the thief, build a gate around destruction and lead to life, and I mean life abundant. It is a lack of discernment and the faulty idea of "tolerance" today that has left many lives a wasteland of destruction and despair.

Jesus knows that we have desires and needs and addresses them by saying "Seek first His kingdom and His righteousness and all of these things will be added to you." He did not say, "Don't have those desires" but, rather keep those desires in proper perspective after all, a man's life does consist of the things which he possesses.

The desire for benefit, value and something bigger and better is a desire placed within us by God. That is how we are motivated. We all tend to move in the direction of what we see as "valuable". Denying that we have these desires and needs destroys the ability to live and we become a mere shadow of what God intended for us to be.

A person told me that this book is part Billy Graham and part Zig Ziglar. Well, I don't know, maybe it is. What I can tell you is that it is from the heart and I want what is best for YOU.

Wisdom must precede warfare and virtue is what comes before victory. I hope you find wisdom and discernment in the pages of this book to help you get your poop in a group!

gambling *for life*

SWINGING THE ODDS IN YOUR FAVOR
FOR MORE MONEY AND GREAT SEX

don't be a rube.

"Everything should be as simple as possible, but no simpler."

-Albert Einstein

"To give prudence to the naïve, to the youth knowledge and discretion, a wise man will hear and increase in learning, And a man of understanding will acquire wise counsel."

-King Solomon's Book of Wisdom Proverbs 1:4-6

What the heck is a "rube" you might ask. A rube is more of a slang term that probably came from one or all of the following. Rube Goldberg was a cartoonist who made unnecessarily intricate and complicated machines for doing simple tasks. A Rubicon is the point at which any action when taken, commits the person to a further particular course of action that cannot be avoided. Jumping in the river just before the waterfall would be an example. A "rube" as defined in an online dictionary is an awkward, inexperienced, unsophisticated and naive person. In gambling terms, the rube is typically the first one out of the poker game.

So, "Don't be a Rube" is a polite way of saying don't be an idiot, don't be naïve and don't be a fool. This short book is primarily aimed at those who see themselves as infinitely wise and all-knowing; most commonly known as "teenagers", "young people" or "20-somethings". They think they have it all figured out and have the world by the tail. It is a great feeling to have; I remember it well, like it was yesterday in fact, and in many ways it was.

I am missing pieces of my life because of the choices I made. Yes, I too was a "rube." Who am I kidding, I still am in many respects!

However, I feel compelled to share some thoughts in the hope that just one person may actually learn from my screw ups and avoid the pain that I had to endure. At the very least, my kids and grandkids will have a written record where they can glean some insight and avoid the potholes and land mines life has set up for them.

There were many things for which I paid too high a price. As Benjamin Franklin told in his short story, *The Whistle*, "You are providing pain for yourself instead of pleasure; you give too much for your whistle." The things that I thought would bring pleasure yielded pain, and in the pursuit of gain I suffered loss. You can get a free .pdf download of *"The Whistle"* at www.getyourpoopinagroup.com/whistle.pdf

Will any of it sink in? I am not sure that it will. I heard many stories when I was younger and thought I knew better. I think younger people are in many ways wiser than I was growing up simply because they have seen more of the fallout from bad choices. The internet has done a wonderful job of exposing lies and falsehood, which is a good thing. People most often act in a way that they believe to be in their best interest. My goal is to help set the record straight with regard to living a truly full life. There are no guarantees in life (except death of course); however, these time-tested truths will definitely swing the odds in your favor. Will people listen? I hope so.

[1]Proverbs 15:2

Regardless, like Jonah who saw a generation of people making foolish choices, I am compelled to try and reach Nineveh. As the great and wise King Solomon said, "the wise make knowledge acceptable¹". So, this is my attempt at trying to be wise.

In the pursuit of truth I may offend a few of you. My desire is, if I do offend you, that you at least see me as sincere. My desire is to offer gain, not pain, and provide you with some bread that I have found as a fellow beggar. I am, like the dentist who reassuringly looks you in the eye and says, "This will hurt a little." You must be willing to suffer through some pain to experience true healing. In this "don't judge" and "be tolerant" environment in which we live, we are allowing many foolish choices to go unchecked by many people who know better.

So here it is; the half dozen things that truly make life worthwhile, or at least the half dozen things to swing the odds in your favor for more money and great sex.

Reegs

the foundation: beliefs, truth and judgment

"You will know the truth, and the truth will make you free."
Jesus in the Gospel of John 8:32

"Do not judge according to appearance, but judge with righteous judgment."
Jesus in the Gospel of John 7:24

"What is truth?"
Pontius Pilate before condemning
Jesus to death in the Gospel of John 18:38

What you believe will have a more profound impact on your life than anything else. It doesn't even matter so much if what you believe is true. If you believe it to be, you will act on it regardless of its accuracy.

Thus, it is so vitally important to examine your beliefs and to understand where they come from. They directly and profoundly impact your behavior, and behavior affects results. Belief itself is neutral. Belief is what you think is true. You will always act in a manner consistent with what you believe to be true at the time.

How do you know what you believe? Simply look at your actions and they will clearly tell you what you believe to be true.

The "formula" looks like this:

> belief affects behavior
> behavior affects results
>
> _____
>
> to change results you must change behavior
> changing behavior requires a change in beliefs

That is what belief really is and what it does. Simple right?

Here's where it gets a little tricky. Are your beliefs helping or hurting you?

Some are easy to spot.

For example, I believe I can touch a red hot stove with my bare hand and not get burned. I can be very sincere and even completely convince myself of the truth of that belief, only to get severely burned once I put the belief into action.

Where did that belief come from? Who knows? Maybe it came from a well-intentioned friend, a religion show on T.V., a movie, or a book. It doesn't really matter where it came from. The point is that we are influenced by all sorts of things and those inputs affect my beliefs.

The results proved it to be false. I got burned with that faulty belief.

We all believe things that we think are true and will help us. Beliefs are shaped by a "grid" or "filter" that we all have. Today, the sophisticated call this grid a "paradigm". It is basically what you use to determine right and wrong, good and bad. Your paradigm is what you use to judge what is true.

Yes, you read correctly. I said judge what is true.

truth

"I want the truth!"
"You can't handle the truth!"
Jack Nicholson & Tom Cruise in "A Few Good Men"

I hate to burst your bubble, rube, but there is truth and truth can be known. What is more, everyone judges everything all the time. There is no getting around it. This notion that there is no truth or truth is relative is the epitome of stupidity, or at least the people proclaiming there is no such thing as truth must think you an idiot for believing it (or be idiots themselves).

Let me illustrate how preposterous the argument is in the following example:

Mr. Smartee Pants Intellectual (Mr. SPI): "There is no such thing as truth. You may believe one thing and I believe something else, therefore, truth is relative to the one believing it and it is different for everyone."

Rube: "Wow that makes sense. You must be really smart."

Reegs: "So, what you are saying is that there is no such thing as truth, right?"

Mr. SPI: "That's right, there is no such thing as truth and even if there was, you couldn't know it anyway."

Reegs: "If that is correct then how do I know what you are saying is true?"

Mr. SPI: "Well, uh, you know what I mean."

Rube: "Hey, that's right. If I can't know truth, how do I know what you are saying is true?"

Mr. SPI: "Reegs is just confusing things because he has an agenda to promote etc. etc. etc........."

See how naïve the comment "there's no such thing as truth" really is? The philosophy people call this a "contradictory statement." You can never know something is wrong without having an absolute truth to measure it against. It is like saying that all pens write with blue ink, but some write with red ink.

There are only three options when a contradictory statement is made: (1) you are wrong, (2) I am wrong, (3) we are both wrong. But, we cannot both be right.

The real issue is that there is truth. In fact, there is absolute truth and people defend their absolute truths tooth and nail. Look at the theory of evolution being taught in schools. That theory taught as "truth" even though there are other theories that have more credibility, even though evolution has been shot full of holes. Try to introduce another theory in the public school and you will have the AFL CIO on you so fast it will make your head spin.

People are not interested in the truth; only in defending what they believe is true. Never mind the fact that the theory of evolution will most likely be put on the same shelf as "the world is flat belief" of earlier generations. (see the movie "Expelled, No Intelligence Allowed" or "Evolution, The Lie")

The fact is that it is the truth that will set you free.

> if you do not believe that there is truth and
> it can be known then you are destined to live
> in the slavery of another

That's right, you are destined to be a slave. Specifically, you will be a slave to the one who defines the truth for you.

Truth is like the compass on a sailboat. It is only by adhering strictly to the compass that the captain can steer away from the shore. Without the truth of the compass he is a slave to the shore and can never be free to explore the world.

the truth is more than convenient
tests for truth

Remember that beliefs are based on what is thought to be true and people use many different tests for truth. For example, an atheist (a person who does not believe in God) will most likely use pragmatism as his primary test for truth. Pragmatism is a straightforward way of looking at things. Is it practical? What will be the results? He is most likely to ask, "Does this belief 'work' for meeting my needs?"

The problem with pragmatism is that 'success' is not truth. Results do not establish what is true, but simply what happens to work. Results may have been accidental or evil. For example, being honest on one's tax returns may be economically painful but right. Economic gain by oppressing the poor might work, but it's not right.

Truth is the way things actually are. It is undeniable.

That you are reading this book right now is an example of a true undeniable statement.

People that want to confuse the simplicity of truth and what it is typically have an agenda to promote and usually are trying to hide something sinister.

In addition, strong, bitter and emotional words are generally an indication of flimsy argument. Things that won't stand on the basis of truth must be defended on the basis of emotion and deception.

One of my favorite quotes on truth is:

> *"The truth is incontrovertible.*
> *Malice may attack.*
> *Ignorance may deride it.*
> *But, in the end there it is."*
> Sir Winston Churchill

In our earlier example, in the end, my hand got burned. The truth is, when you put your hand on a hot stove, you get burned. Notice the simple truth in that?

It is easy enough for a two year old to understand.

Here is one guaranteed truth. You will die someday. That my friend, you can take to the bank. It is a truth guaranteed.

Instead of exclaiming that there is no such thing as truth, what people should really be asking is. "How do you determine what the truth is?"

You determine truth with judgment. You must judge between right and wrong, good and bad, profit and loss.

For a more complete discussion of truth and tests for truth go to www.getyourpoopinagroup.com/truth

judgment

There seems to be a lot of fuzzy thinking going on with the idea of judgment. Nevertheless, judgment in itself is neutral. You can have either good judgment or bad judgment. Saying judgment is bad is like saying money is bad. Money is neutral. You can do good or bad things with it. It is the same way with judging.

For example,

Mr. SPI: "You shouldn't judge."

Rube: "Oh, yeah. I see what you mean. That might hurt someone's feelings."

Reegs: "Wait a minute. You're saying I shouldn't judge?"

Mr. SPI: "That's right, you shouldn't judge."

Reegs: "Isn't that a judgment?"

Mr. SPI: "Uh, well, yeah, but, hey, who are you anyway?"

Reegs: "I am a father trying to help my kids think through the idiocy of your statements."

Judgment is necessary for survival. I must have good judgment to drive my car. If I don't, I might get in an accident and kill myself or someone else. It was my poor judgment earlier in the chapter that got my hand burned.

Judgment has gotten a real bad reputation as of late. While good people have checked themselves out of the debate for fear of being viewed as "judgmental", evil has been running wild and destroying all that is true, honorable, right, pure, lovely, of good repute, excellent and worthy of praise.

But, what has gotten so many rubes off track is a verse from the Bible that keeps getting quoted over and over and over again.

The verse is in the book of Matthew and it says, "Judge not lest you be judged." The problem is that it is taken completely out of context, and if one would actually go back and read the entire passage one would conclude that

Jesus did not say "Do not judge," but rather Jesus was saying "Don't be a hypocrite."

See, the religious leaders of the day had some faulty thinking about judgment as well, so Jesus said, "Take the log out of your own eye before trying to take the speck out of your brother's eye." He did not say, take the log out of your own eye and leave the speck in your brother's.

No, you have to see the situation, determine right from wrong and then act in a manner consistent with your beliefs and judgment.

Remember Rube, if you repeat a lie long enough eventually people will begin to believe it. Judgment is not the problem. It is like money, guns or matches. It can be used for good or evil.

No, judgment is not the problem. Deception and lies are the problem. Any judgment based on a lie is doomed to failure.

For a more complete discussion on judging go to www.getyourpoopinagroop.com/judgement for a free .pdf download on the subject.

common sense moment:

If you don't stand for something you will fall for anything.

If you don't think there is something worth standing for you will fall for anything.

If you don't know what you should stand for you will fall for anything

.

With no beliefs, no truth and no judgment you will quickly fall prey to the world and its system to fleece you for everything you've got. They will take your time, your money and your life. You will in fact become a slave. Not to think so is naïve.

> without truth and judgment you will become
> the slave of another

With regard to judgment of other people's actions you must keep a few things in mind. You can never really know someone else's motives unless they tell you, and even then you don't know for sure. So, it is best never to judge someone's motives.

Judgment of others should be based on two criteria. First, always, always, always, have the other person's best interest in mind. This, by the way is the best definition of love that I have ever heard.

> love is not simply a feeling. love is a verb.
> love is active. love is having the best
> interest of the other person at heart.

Listen to me here if you are a Bible-believing Christian. I don't mind you condemning my soul to hell for my sins as long as you do it with care and concern for me as evidenced by a tear and not with a smile or with hatred.

Second, judgment of another should always be based on the Jim Rayburn model of "earning the right to be heard." The better a relationship I have with someone the stronger I can be. If I don't know you that well it is very difficult for me to help because I don't have the relationship required for good judgment.

Finally, I am continually amazed at my capacity to delude myself. As such, I find it infinitely helpful to have another person spot errors in judgment and to see me in a different light. Because I have blind spots, I require others to help me see them. Without the judgment, confrontation and concern from other people (especially from my wife) I would be lost.

I tend to either see myself better than I am, or to see myself worse than I am. It is through other people that I begin to see my strengths and weaknesses more clearly. I cannot do it in a vacuum with any accuracy or truth.

A proper response to the judgment of others should be to listen and hear what they are saying. Why are they saying that? Is it true? What is the basis for their discernment. A younger man should be subject his elders. Listen, learn and grow. In business this is called a 360° review. We ALL have blind spots and need help to see them.

So. You know where I stand. Beliefs are based on what you judge to be true and you will act on those beliefs as long as you see them as helping you improve benefits or avoid suffering loss.

Because I am mostly concerned with the young "Rubes" of the day (and because it is my book), I will focus on what I believe to be on the minds of most young men. Based on observation, conversation and my own life experience, the primary motivators for young men are money and sex.

Those two (knee jerk) motivators ultimately used for meeting other needs like power, respect, etc. Young men act most quickly and effectively in the direction getting the girl or getting the money.

Don't believe me? Look at the commercials on TV and look at who these "Rubes" idolize.

Other motivators like respect, wisdom, long life, happiness, etc. often come into play when the money and sex desire is clarified.

Pareto's Principle

An Italian economist named Vilfredo Pareto observed *that 80% of income in Italy went to 20% of the population. It is a common rule of thumb in business; e.g., "80% of your sales comes from 20% of your clients."*

I have also found that the 80/20 rule is very helpful in life. "Pareto's Principle" as it is called can save you much head and heartache as you work through life.

What that means is that there is generally a handful of things that make most of the difference in any scenario. For example, if you want to be an effective Christian you could create a list of things that will help you in that regard. The list could include (1) reading the Bible for yourself, (2) spending an adequate amount of time in prayer, (3) applying what you read to your life (4) teaching others who are new in the faith (5) holding yourself accountable with other believers, and (6) being generous with time and resources. I could make the list as long or short as I choose, but the point is that if your focus on a handful of things (i.e. the 20%) they become more manageable and allow you to create order and positive results (i.e. the 80%) in your life.

The goal then is to target those things that make the most difference and focus on doing those things first.

The rest of the book will focus on the half dozen things that promote great sex, help you get more money and have a long healthy life. I offer them with the scars and stories that attest to their accuracy. What I mean is, that by pursuing sex and money with blatant disregard for these half dozen things, you are swinging your odds away from truly achieving the thing in which you desire.

In fact, you make it more difficult and potentially impossible to achieve what it is that you truly want in life.

I challenge you; test them on your own! Instead of getting drunk and driving your car to see if you can pass a breath test from a police officer, learn from other people's experience first. It saves the time and money lost when learning it on your own.

But, hey, if you believe it is better to make the same mistakes others have already made, -feel free. Go right ahead. Then you will be able to tell a story to others about your own scars and losses, filled with remorse, regret and life long consequences.

So, what are the handful of things that I have found that have the biggest impact in life? Here they are:

marriage
spirituality
wisdom
health
work
wealth

Of course, there are a handful of things that support each of those and that is the basis for the rest of the book.

I hope you enjoy it and glean some helpful insights that will spare you some pain and accrue some added benefit to your life account.

"If there is one thing upon this earth that mankind love and admire better than another, it is a brave man, -- it is the man who dares to look the devil in the face and tell him he is a devil."
James A. Garfield

marriage

"Everything you do will fail until you do right by me."
-Celie, The Color Purple

Let your fountain be blessed, And rejoice in the wife of your youth.
King Solomon to his son

*"It's not true that married men live longer than single men.
It only SEEMS longer."*
-Anonymous

"Let marriage be held in honor among all."

Hebrews 13:4

If you are really interested in money and sex, it is in your best interest to get married. Being married gives you the best chance for meeting both of those desires. Skeptical? I don't blame you,

I am sure that all of you have heard the story about the man, traveling on an overcrowded train, who was double booked with a woman in the sleeping car. There was a bunk bed so he took the top bunk and she took the lower.

In the middle of the night he woke with a slight chill. Knocking quietly on the lower bunk, he said,

"Excuse me ma'am. I hate to disturb you, but it is a little chilly on this train. Would you mind reaching over and handing me the blanket?"

She replied, "You know. It is only the two of us in this sleeping car, and we will most likely never see each other again. Why don't we just pretend that we are married for tonight?

Surprised and excited the man responded, "Well that sounds like a great idea!"

She said, "Great, get your own darn blanket."

A few moments later, he farted.

That story does a pretty good job of taking the temperature of what Americans think about marriage. In fact, that is probably a little on the positive side of what people think about marriage today. The world portrays marriage in such a bad light, it is no wonder people are cynical about it. Especially young people.

While I was working on this book I would randomly ask a variety of folks just to see how they thought about marriage. One day, I overheard a lady talking to some college students about marriage. She said, "Whatever you do, don't get married before you are 30 years old." She emphatically declared. "You have to give yourself time to find out who you are."

When she left, I asked the question, "So what do you guys think about marriage?"

The one young lady said, "In all honesty, I'm cynical. I am in a long term relationship, but marriage frankly scares me."

I said, "It's like playing Russian Roulette isn't it? You just know that there is a bullet in one of those chambers."

"Exactly!" Her friend exclaimed.

While I may not totally agree with the time frame, (waiting until thirty seems a little excessive), I think the lady has a good point. You have to give yourself some time to sort things out a bit in order to be better prepared to share your life with someone else. I know that there are stories of high school sweethearts that got married young and lived happily ever after spending 70 years married to the same person. But if you get married prior to age 25 the odds are against you making it.

I think one of the most devastating things affecting marriage is the misconceptions that exist around it. If you look at the world around you, there is nothing positive to be found in marriage. However, that is simply not what the data actually shows.

the marriage revolving door?

Contrary to popular belief, marriage has many positive benefits, not the least of which has to do with money and sex. Statistics, research reports, data, even popular magazines show this. Here are a few facts on marriage benefits:

1. **live longer** - on average married folks live 7 years longer than non-married;
2. **make more money** - average income is $15k more per year;
3. **have more money** - average net worth is $100k higher.
4. **give more money** - average give $5k more
5. **report happier lives;**
6. **have sex more often;**
7. **have better sex;**
8. **have better attitude;**
9. **have better health and least likely to be in poor health** (especially ages 18-44) and least likely to be restricted in some way (especially age 65+)
10. **married people were healthier for nearly every measure of health.**[1]

It doesn't matter where you look either. It can be at a conservative church service or a left-wing liberal women's lib magazine like Cosmo, they all report the same thing. Marriage gives both men and women the most of what they are looking for in terms of money and sex.

All things being equal, marriage holds the key to success in ALL areas of life. As Amy Hymowitz, in her book Marriage and Caste in America states, "It's not just poverty that's at stake here. You can control for education, for income, for race, for number of siblings, but children from single parent families – both as a result of divorce and as a result of non-marriage – are more prone to just about every social problem: school failure, delinquency, crime, early pregnancy, emotional difficulties and a host of other problems."

She continues, "Marriage, I think you can argue when you look at the numbers, now poses an even larger social divide than race."

[1]CDC, Advanced Data from Vital and Health Statistics Number 351 December 15, 2004

Yet, the jokes, ridicule and lies about marriage run rampant.

The attitudes toward marriage do nothing to help the situation either. There is a generation of kids being raised that firmly believe that marriage is at best a "crap shoot", that will be more trouble than it is worth and that it really isn't all that important anyway.

But, is that really true?

I can't tell you how many guys I talk to that have either gotten divorced and regretted it, came from a divorced home and hate their parents for it, vowing never to let that happen to their family, or are now considering it and think divorce will give them more money, more sex and a happier life.

Every piece of data you find says the exact OPPOSITE is true. Divorce for any kind of benefit is almost always a lie, which is probably why God says it is one of the things He hates.[2]

But is divorce really as certain as we tend to believe? Are there things I can do to swing the odds in my favor for a successful marriage? The data suggest that there are.

The following is from Matthew Bramlett and William Mosher, the National Center for Health and Statistics: Cohabitation, Marriage, Divorce and Remarriage in the United States.

Factors	% Decrease in Risk of Divorce
Annual income $50k+ vs. <$25k	-30%
Having baby 7 mos+ after marriage vs. before marriage	-24%
Marrying over 25 vs under 18	-24%
Own family intact vs divorced parents	-14%
Religious affiliation vs none	-14%
Some college vs HS dropout	-13%

[2]Malachi 2:16 "For I hate divorce," says the LORD, the God of Israel, "

They conclude *"If you are a reasonably well-educated person with a decent income, come from an intact family, are religious, and marry after age 25 without having a baby first, your chances of divorce are very low indeed."*

So, we now know the odds of protecting from divorce. But, what are some of the keys to a good marriage? The following are what I have found to be the most beneficial to not only surviving marriage but most beneficial to a thriving marriage.

money
spirituality/religion
wisdom/education
sex
health
work

The most important thing to have if you are going to have the best shot of a good marriage is to have similar values. The single most important value to hold in high regard is the value that you place on your marriage.

You see, there is no one who will support you in marriage today. But, everyone will support you in divorce. Marriage takes work. A great marriage is hard to find, which is why it is so valuable. The scarcity makes it valuable. The more valuable it is the harder it is to acquire.

One divorced guy at a party said that "marriage stinks, everyone I know is either divorced, has a crappy marriage or hates it. Except one couple I know, marriage is for the birds."

He spoke with such conviction, sincerity and passion that it was easy to become captivated by his speech.

Yet, about a year later the same guy at a different party said that "he is lonely and bored most weekends. He would give his right arm to have a great marriage."

The ironic thing is, it may cost you your right arm. That's about what it costs. But, that cost is still less than the alternative, and the profit derived from it pales in comparison to the cost.

The grass is NEVER greener on the other side of the fence. The grass is always greener where you water it.

Or as Mrs. Regan (my mom) says, "the grass is always greener because it has been watered with someone else's tears."

No, marriage is not easy, but then again neither is exercising and working out. But, like a healthy body, a great marriage is worth the effort. You can focus on paying the price for something; that's fine. But, I would rather focus on the benefits that I reap from the effort.

marriage and money

Some facts.

According to the "Millionaire Next Door" by Dr. Thomas J. Stanley, "the largest percentage of millionaires are still married to their first wife." To increase your chances of being a millionaire, get married and stay married.

I remember my parents always saying that two people can live as cheaply as one as long as one doesn't eat. (Yes, mom and dad, I did pay attention.) This happens to be a key point.

When a working-man and a working-woman get married they have dual income and only one household to support. If a newly married couple takes advantage of that, prior to having children, a nest egg can be started to set them on the path to financial freedom. As I show in the chapter on money, the early years of savings and investment are critically important to long-term success.

However, this only seems to hold true for married folks. For some reason the two that live together (i.e. "shack up") do not get the same advantage as those who are married.

Married men in particular make significantly more money than do bachelors.

When it comes to earnings, for men, getting and keeping a wife may be as important as getting an education.

To have the best chance for earning a higher income get married and stay married. I have heard business owners say that as soon as a person gets married they hold that person in higher regard and will take that into consideration during performance reviews, increasing the amount of raise in pay. There is something about a married person that enhances their perception, wisdom and responsibility. Married employees tend to be happier, more stable and effective in their work compared to unhappy, less stable and ineffective employees.

The flip side of this is to look at what divorce does. The average divorce costs $50,000 (most on attorneys fees) according to an article in the NY Sun, May 17, 2005.

In fact, a single divorce costs state and local governments about $30,000 based on such things as higher use of food stamps and public housing as well as increased bankruptcies and juvenile delinquency. In 2002 it is estimated that the 10.4 million divorces cost the tax-payers over $30 billion.[3]

Common sense tells you that divorce destroys wealth. Instead of income going to support one household, divorce forces the support of two through child support and alimony. Instead of the multiplying effect that marriage creates by living together in one household, divorce destroys this benefit and creates a division that erodes and destroys wealth.

marriage and sex

If you are interested in sex, by all means get married! Don't buy into the lie that married people have sex less often than their single counterparts. Nothing could be farther from the truth. After all, wives are easy, as I will soon explain.

Married people consistently report higher frequency and quality in their sex lives than their single and divorced counterparts. What about the "live-in-lovers" who "shack up", as Dr. Laura likes to call it? They do report having

[3]Source, Whitehead B. and Propenoe, D. The State of Our Unions.

sex slightly more often than married people do, but they report enjoying it less.[4]

In, The Case For Marriage, they report that a man having a wife surpasses shacking up by a wide margin. Both a physically and an emotionally satisfying sex life is significantly better than cohabitating or single men and women.

They continue by saying that "'Committed sex is better sex' is a truism among women. What better way for a woman to feel that she is in a committed relationship than when she is married? The more comfortable and familiar a person is with you, the more likely you are to have an intimate relationship with them. Contrary to popular belief, familiarity does more to facilitate ardor than to dampen it."

Let's compare a married man and a single dude looking for 'love'.

After a tough week at work the single guy has to get cleaned up and go hunting for a compatible bedfellow. He will spend time and money looking for "Miss right now". He will get rejected more times than he will succeed and he will (at the least) have to buy drinks for the "prospects" in an attempt to build a "relationship", strong enough to get her in bed with him.

Typically, this will take weeks or longer. Because there is no commitment, it will not last long and the process will again have to be repeated.

A married couple on the other hand can skip the "get to know you phase" and instead focus on the "get to know you even better stage". They can be tired at the end of the week and still have a willing and able body right next to them. This is what I mean by "wives are easy".

Married men report that committed sex is more physically pleasing. This helps to dispel the lie that men find sex more fun with "a new woman". Why is that? Well, as every good athlete knows, "Practice makes perfect." In a married relationship, if you don't do something right, you get to try it again, and again, and again, and again. You don't ever really start over, you just keep growing and building upon what you have already known. The long

---

[4]This is according to Linda Waite and Maggie Gallagher in their book "The Case for Marriage."

time horizon of marriage gives both partners the time and motivation to learn how to please one another. In fact, keeping the long term in perspective can also help put the occasional sexual disappointment into perspective as well.

They continue to say that "sexual pleasure is doubled when it is with someone you love." This makes sense as well. You not only get satisfaction from your own sexual response but from your partner's as well. A selfless approach to sex, is far more likely to bring sexual satisfaction to both men and women.

Married sex is better sex because:[5]

   1. **Proximity-** Sex is easier for married people, because it is more fitted into their everyday lives.

   2. **A long-term contract-** Married people have more incentive to invest time and energy into pleasing their partners, have more time in which to learn how to please them, and are more confident that the gifts they give to their partners will be reciprocated.

   3. **Exclusivity-** Without other sexual outlets, married people put more effort into working out a mutually agreeable sex life than the less committed do.

   4. **Emotional bonding-** In marriage, sex becomes a symbol of the union of the partners, or their commitment to care for each other both in bed and out of it. By giving sex this added meaning, marriage increases the satisfaction men and women draw from sexual activity – both their own and their partners.

marriage and health

> **WARNING!**
> "Not being married can be hazardous
> to your health!"

Married folks report healthier lives than any other social group. Divorce in particular is very hazardous to your health. In fact, according to Professor

[5]Did you know that the only New Testament reason given in the Bible for marriage, is for the sex? In fact, the Apostle Paul said if you really want to serve the Lord, do not get married, but because of the lack of self control with regard to sex, get married! 1 Corinthians 7:1-9

Harold Morowitz of Yale University, he concluded that divorce is about as hazardous to your health as picking up a pack-a-day cigarette habit.[6]

Facts about married people:

Live longer than unmarried by about ten years.

Live healthier lives

Spend less on health care

Are more active

Look about two years younger.

Are safer. Wives as well as husbands are much less likely to be abused physically than single women and men.

Being unmarried can actually be a greater risk to one's life than having heart disease or cancer. In fact, according to Bernard Cohen and I-Sing Lee, who compiled a catalog of risks that increase chances of dying, concluded that for both men and women.

". . . being unmarried is one of the greatest risks that people voluntarily subject themselves to."

marriage and cancer.

Being married in the fight against cancer is the equivalent of being ten years younger. That would be like a 40 year old vs. 50 year old facing the disease. The younger person has a much better chance of beating it than the older person.

In addition, the survival rate of surgery is far greater for married people compared to singles. And when they are discharged, they are 2.5 times more likely to go back home as opposed to going to a nursing home.

Married men and women even feel healthier than those who are divorced, separated or widowed according to research. Wives are 30% more likely to rate their own health excellent or very good than single women and 40% less likely to to say that their health is only fair or poor. Husbands showed simi-

---

[6]Glen Stanton, Why Marriage Matters: Reasons to Believe in Marriage in a Post-modern Society. :Hiding in the Hammond Report" Hospital Practice. Page 211 The Case for Marriage.

lar advantages over unmarried men. Plus, the married are less likely than singles to suffer from long term chronic illness or disabilities.

pay attention fellas!

For men, however, avoiding wedlock is particularly risky business. Three out of ten single, widowed or divorced middle aged men can expect to die before age 65 when they lose their wives. This is a 300% increase in the death rate compared to those who are still married.

The married are more likely to live longer as the following chart illustrates:

	Over 65 Men	Over 65 Women
Married	90% chance	90% chance
Unmarried	67% chance	80% chance

Shacking up, however, does not offer the same protection as marriage does.

The big health difference is between married people and the nonmarried, not between people who live alone and those who don't.

A marriage license is more than "just a piece of paper" as far as your health and longevity are concerned.

A marriage relationship intertwines two people like a couple living together cannot. It is this increased sense of responsibility for another that distinguishes marriages from other alternatives like cohabitation. This in turn, increases the likelihood of making better choices about your life and well-being, which is due to the increased obligations and commitment level to the relationship and its success. This is exactly the reason why people shack up to begin with, to AVOID those commitments and obligations.

All men, regardless of age or amount of alcohol normally consumed prior to marriage, imbibe less once they are married. In fact, all "self-destructive behaviors" improve with marriage. This includes drug use, driving fast, getting into fights and cigarette smoking. The moment a man says, "I do" (or even sets the wedding date), he holds death and the Grim Reaper at bay.

Almost any marriage is good for your health but a good marriage is particularly healthy. The better the marriage the bigger the benefits. Marriage even reduces the chances of catching the common cold. One great way to minimize medical expenditures is to shift the money and time spent on doctors and prescriptions and use it instead to improve your marriage. A date with your wife not only provides long term health benefits but the immediate short term gratification is not all that bad either.

There is something about the marriage bed and the kitchen table that help couples ward off physical illness.

Prescription: *It takes two. Get married and stay married then call me in the morning.*

marriage and wisdom

It's smart to get married and stay married, especially for the children. Wisdom is not the same as education, but children of married parents get more schooling than children in single parent families.

This education gap begins early and continues into adulthood. Being raised in a single-parent home doubles the risk of becoming a high school drop out, while children whose parents stay married are more likely to go to college.

Why is this? Mostly it has to do with time and money. Married parents have more of both to help their kids. There is less disruption in the home compared to single and divorced parents. Because married parents have more money they are more likely to send their kids to a better college. Additionally, the student will most likely have less debt upon graduating.

The psychological wellbeing of kids is higher among the married as well. They are much less likely to be depressed, exhibiting better emotional health.

[5]James 4:17

This in turn helps them think more clearly and at least have the appearance of being smarter.

Maybe that is why married folks tend to have a higher IQ than non-married. People who are wise get married before having children because they are preparing their children to carry on a way of life. It has been said that "even birds will build a nest before laying eggs."

It simply makes sense. Low income single mothers with limited education see things fundamentally different from their educated and married peers. Educated women believe that marriage is the best institution for raising children.

> This "Marriage Gap" is the primary reason for the self-perpetuating disparity among education and income in America.

The upward mobility is all but lost on a low income single mother. When America chose to believe that marriage before children was optional, the poor were the hardest hit. They not only lost a steadfast partner, a second income, and a trusted babysitter, they lost a traditional arrangement that reinforced precisely the qualities that they needed for upward mobility. Qualities needed more than ever in a tough new knowledge economy.

marriage and religion

There is a strong correlation between marriage and religious activity. Even though the divorce rates are the same for "Christians" or other religious groups, those who get married and stay married report "the religious faith" as a strong cause for the success of their marriage. It takes a strong belief and faith to persevere through difficult times, which occur in all marriages.

A belief system based on truths, that supports marriage and the family (such as Biblical Christianity) is indispensable to help through tough times. You must have faith in something bigger than yourself or your spouse to believe in. It requires faith and work to be successful. An ancient script even says, "faith without work's is useless, dead in fact"[7] You can believe some-thing all day long, but fail to put that belief to work and you will get killed.

Someone much smarter than me said, "You can be on the right track but you will get run over by the train if you just sit there and do nothing."

Marriage and Work

Want a job? Get married. Well maybe it is not that simple, but married people are much more likely to be working than those who are not married. There are some obvious reasons for this. First, the desire and necessity to support a wife and family is very strong in good men. Second, married men tend to be more responsible, healthy and wise so they are better prospects for employers to hire. After all, what employer wouldn't want to hire a depend-able, healthy and smart man to help him become even more profitable?

By the way, there is one other side benefit to marriage not typically reported on:

marriage makes people happier too

Married folks report being happier than any other group of people. But, does marriage make you happy or do happy people get married? Why are married people so much healthier mentally and happier emotionally than those who are not married? Maybe it is easier for happy and healthy people to find a mate. It could be, but the research clearly shows that it does not explain the huge advantage in emotional and mental health that married peo-ple enjoy.

Regardless of their mental state prior to marriage, when people got mar-ried their mental health improved – consistently and substantially. The con-verse is also true, when people divorced or separated, they suffered substan-tial deterioration in mental and emotional well being including increases in depression and declines in happiness.

---

[7]James 2:20 But are you willing to recognize, you foolish fellow, that faith without works is useless?
James 2:26 For just as the body without the spirit is dead, so also faith without works is dead.

> Holding all other variables constant. Married people
> are 18% more likely to say that they are very happy
> compared to unmarried.
> Arthur C. Brooks, Gross National Happiness

Those who dissolved a marriage reported less personal mastery, less positive relations with others, less purpose in life and less self acceptance than their married peers.

By the way, divorce is much harder on a woman in terms of depression, self-acceptance and personal growth.

The message is clear. Having a person in your life who is committed for better or worse, in sickness and health, makes people happier and healthier.

Marriage is a good thing to be in and to bet on – especially if you are interested in money and sex.

Now, the question is what are you doing to become that man, or woman worth marrying? The next five chapters are dedicated to answering that question.

> *". . . one of the best ways to become modestly wealthy in America*
> *has nothing to do with investments:*
> *Get married and stay married."*

Scott Burns, Dallas Morning News

spirituality

*The spirit has fifty-times the strength and staying power
of brawn and muscle."*
Mark Twain

"The Spirit is willing but the flesh is weak."
Jesus The Bible Matthew 26:41

*"What comes in our minds when we think about God
is the most important thing about us."*
A.W. Tozer

Over the past three decades George Lucas has been fascinating us with
his epic story Star Wars. The response of the world was truly amazing for he
was able to capture the hearts and minds through the classic good vs. evil
story of a young man overcoming obstacles to win the day. The hero and
heroine were alive and well and our sense of justice was satisfied when evil
was defeated.

Star Wars re-introduced a religious component to the masses through the mysterious "force." Before every great battle or teaching moment it was customary to focus on the "force" and how it flows through you. This was by no means a new idea, for eastern religions and philosophies have been teaching that for years. It is basically a pantheistic view of the world, or a view that there is no one God or right way to do things, just some mystical "force" that binds us all together.

A similar idea was presented in the Lord of The Rings series where the "One Ring" would bind them all. The point of all of this is to illustrate how we are all spiritual beings. We know that there is something out there, but we are not quite sure how it all fits together.

The ancient Greeks taught three basic things to focus on; your mind, your body and your spirit.

Mind, body and spirit. I kind of like that. It's simple, straight forward and can get my hands around it. It makes sense too. Clearly my mind is not my body and my body is not my spirit and although not as clear, my spirit is not my mind. They seem to be three different but, intimately connected components to my life.

I have found that to be true in my life as well. In fact, they all must be given proper attention or I will soon fall out of balance in my life. For, if I spend too much time just on the spiritual side of life, my mind and my body will quickly atrophy. Likewise if I spend all of my time on the body, my spirit and mind will suffer.

It takes all three and all three require attention and feeding.

I started with spirit because I think that is ultimately where we all are. There is a longing in our spirit, a demand in fact, that must be made full or at the minimum, contented for the moment.

You can see how important the spirit is in any conflict. Take a boxing match or a battle in war. Once the spirit of the enemy has been suitably deflated, the body is right behind it. As soon as the spirit is gone, the body might as well be dead. In fact, many times it is. That is how it is described in medicine. "His spirit has left him." Then they pronounce him dead.

Let's look at "the force" for example. It provides power and control. Even the evil Darth Vader said, "If you only knew the power of the dark side of the force." We all are seeking a "power" source or enthusiasm in our spirit.

Enthusiasm, by the way is a great word. One of my favorite authors is Charlie "T" Jones. He says that "enthusiasm makes the difference." Did you know that enthusiasm is the connecting of Greek words that means "God within you?"

So enthusiasm and motivation are simply ways of saying "your spirit is moving you to do something." We all want that right?

The other thing that we want, especially in today's world, is regeneration and renewal, or refreshment at least. Gatorade has a commercial where the athlete is working up a sweat. As he begins to sweat, a colorful liquid begins to ooze from his pores. The "sweat" is actually the Gatorade beverage seeping through his skin. During a break, he refuels with another Gatorade. The commercial ends by asking, "Is IT in you?" The idea being that Gatorade will not only give you refreshment but is the actual fuel driving power and performance.

Is IT in you? What is in you? What do you believe? Is it true? What do you put your faith in? Is that working?

Hollywood and the marketers on Madison avenue know all about this longing in your spirit. They know it is both real and powerful. They know it is true and they use that to sell a promise connected to their product, hoping to fill or at least make content your spirit's calling within you.

But, is that true? Does what they sell truly provide what you want or is it simple salt water only making you thirsty for more and more?

Remember that faith and believe are the same word. One is a noun and the other is a verb. It is the acceptance that something is real or true and that what I have faith in or believe to be true is good or will be effective.

The opposite of belief is doubt. Doubt suspects something is untrue, unlikely or insincere; it is unconvinced or uncertain.

Everyone has faith and beliefs. Everyone of those beliefs has been established in our lives to either help us to gain profit or to avoid loss. The mental scales are weighing (judging) right and wrong, good and evil, profit and loss all the time, every day. If you don't like the words "profit" and "loss", use "hope" and "despair" or "pleasure" and "pain". Whatever the words, we all make decisions this way. That is how we are created.

Now, some beliefs are true, some are false. Some are good for us and some are bad. It is the refinement and testing of those beliefs that can either lead us to men of strength and maturity or to boys of weakness and perpetual adolescence.

The weighing of right and wrong or the testing, is based on how you validate truth. For the believer, the truth scales should be based on the Bible.

Jesus said, I am the way the truth and the life.

Jesus is the author and is perfect truth.

The truth will set you free.

The Bible records many new beliefs Jesus taught to the religious leaders of the day. He knew that they would not be accepted as truth and that He as well as His ideas would be rejected. That is why He started many of His talks by saying things like, "Truly, truly I tell you." In fact He starts speaking that way 83 times in His talks to people. He knew that they would have a hard time believing what He was saying.

For your faith and beliefs to be effective they must be based on truth. Otherwise, they are ultimately doomed to fail you.

The Christian believes that everyone is born into a sinful world and has a sinful nature due to the original sin of Adam and Eve in the Garden of Eden.

Belief or faith is created by God. We all believe something. Even the agnostic who claims that he doesn't believe in anything believes in agnosticism. Everyone has faith and beliefs. Faith was given to all of us by God. He is the author of faith.

Faith/belief also implies that we have the capacity to choose. We get to choose whatever we want. Our faith/beliefs will be effected by whatever we expose ourselves to and by what our truth scale leads us to believe based on influence and experience.

Sin and separation from God stems from my unwillingness to believe Jesus and believe what He said is true. My human faith and beliefs are perverted and warped. I try to fulfill my needs on my own accord. I want to determine what is best for me.

It is this deciding-for-myself-what-I-think-is-best that got Adam and Eve into trouble in the beginning. They wanted to decide and did not want God to decide for them. In order to get back to a right relationship with God, I must believe that God is good and has my best interest at heart. I need to align myself with God and admit that He knows best. He knows better than I. I must believe what He says in His Bible and that He rewards faithfulness.

This "realignment" by God can only be tested and made true by the Bible. Jesus is not only the author, but He is also the perfecter of faith and beliefs. There are many "beliefs" and you can put your faith in many things. But, it is only through Christ Jesus that these are tested for truth.

Spending time in the Bible will realign our beliefs, thoughts and faith, so we have assurance that we are being true.

The three tools that God has left the Believer for testing and examining truth are the Bible, the Holy Spirit and Godly people.

Godly men must be tested for accuracy of truth as well however through the Bible, so also to determine if it is truly the Holy Spirit speaking to me.

Jesus' encouraged the testing of the spirit and the testing of teachers when He said, "Beloved, do not believe every spirit, but test the spirits to see whether they are from God, because many false prophets have gone out into the world."[2]

How does the Believer test (judge) what is right? The same way that the men of a town called Berea did. They searched the Scriptures daily to see if these things were so.[8]

So, we all have a mixture of accurate and erroneous beliefs. No one has it perfect. The perfection of beliefs can only be found through Jesus as defined in the Bible.

Believing what Jesus said is the only way to have a full life here on earth and in the life to come. That is the blessed hope and assurance that He promises.

Both a full life here and in eternity. Wow. That is a pretty good deal.

But, you must believe what He says. That requires a change in your thinking. You must choose between God and man. Who gets to decide what is right and wrong?

Either He is or He isn't. There can be no middle ground. By the way, the evidence of your choice can be found in what you DO. For the Christian obedience is the proof of the faith.

Contrary to what you may believe. God does want what is best for you. He is God and can do all things. He came that you may have life and have it abundantly.

But, He says that we are little children. He promises that He will train and discipline the ones He loves just like a parent will discipline a child or a coach will discipline an athlete to become even better.

Discipline always has the best interest of the other person at heart and never seems pleasant at the time. But, when the time of testing comes, that is when discipline pays off.

---

[8] 1 John 4:1   [3] Acts 17:11

We do not know what is in our best interest just like a child does not know what is in his best interest. A child wants to play in the street. A child wants to eat candy all day long. A child will throw a temper tantrum if he doesn't get his way.

The only reason he throws the temper tantrum is he can't see that what the parent says actually is what is best for the child.

One of the first commands of God tells children to obey their parents. Why?

Not for the parents sanity, but because it is in the best interest of the child. God says that a child is to obey so that he may have long life and so that things may go well with you.

A parent says, eat your vegetables, study your books, stay out of the street, work hard, etc.

A child has limited knowledge of consequences so they rebel. A wise parent will try and make the knowledge that they have acceptable to the child. They will try and explain things, but early on they must be disciplined without much explanation because the child cannot understand.

God is the same way. He has told us things in His Bible but, we have trouble understanding them because He is God and we are only human. We are temporal focused and God is eternally focused. We need spiritual glasses to see the spiritual. We can't understand because we do not now how to discern spiritual things.

I continue to discipline my child until the child finally comes to me and says, dad, I want to know more, I believe you, teach me your ways.

But, that child will never come to me if he doesn't see benefit in doing so. He will forever rebel and do things his own way.

God says, here I am. Listen to me. Follow my ways and I will give you life abundant. Nobody really believes that so they play games and do things on their own. You see it everyday. Lies and hypocrisy.

The Bible promises life. God gives us a manual for successful living here on earth and for the life to come.

Yet, somehow today it is taught that all of the "juice" or benefits for the Christian are in eternity. Seeking temporal rewards or benefits are wrong for the true believer.

God says	Satan says
Gain is good.	Gain is bad.

OK, gain is good, but my way is better than God's way.

That is the fundamental lie. It used to be that God's way as defined in the Bible is good for gain. It may be difficult at times, especially in the beginning. But, that is no different from anything else.

For example, Discipline of diet and exercise to a healthy and improved body; Discipline of study and preparation to a wise and intelligent brain; Discipline of finances and cash flow to a wealth of assets and financial freedom; Discipline of communication with your spouse to a beautiful relationship.

Paul, one of the first teachers of the early Christians said that bodily discipline is of little benefit, but Godly discipline is not only profitable for this life, but also for the life to come.9

gain or profit

Everyone moves in the direction of their hope. Hope is whatever you determine to be of benefit to or gain for you.

Why does the farmer plant the crops if not for the hope of the harvest. Why does the factory worker go to work except for the promise of the paycheck? Why does the investor buy a stock except for the promise of gain?

Seeking gain or a profit motive is at the heart of everyone. Everyone wants what they believe to be in their best interest.

There are always at least two voices talking in your head. Old cartoons would show the picture of the "good voice" on one shoulder debating with

9 1 Timothy 4:8

the "bad voice" on the other. That is a pretty good reflection of how we relate with our inner thoughts, especially as it relates to our spirit and our body (or flesh).

There is a Spirit that motivates, that encourages, that renews, that regenerates, a Spirit that gives life. There is also a spirit that discourages and takes life. The first focuses on the spirit, the second on the flesh. One is truth, the other is a lie. One will be for your benefit, the other for your harm. It is a battle we must wage every moment of every day.

One "voice" (i.e. spirit) leads to life, the other leads to death. You get to choose which spirit you want to feed, encourage, and make stronger. Both will be calling for attention and feeding. Your decisions about which one to feed and which one to starve will set the sail on your life course. Make no mistake, however, the choice is yours. That's the good news. The bad news is that your choice will affect the journey and outcome of your life.

Some choices will be right, others will not. Sometimes the choice is easy and other times it is not. I can tell you that the longer I have lived the cloudier many things have become. Which is why it is imperative to test the spirits within you with the truth. More so now than ever before I think.

You feel led to do something that you believe is from God. Great. Now test it. How?

Start by asking: Is it the wise thing to do? That question alone will clear up a lot of fuzzy thinking and help you make choices that lead to more life instead of taking life away from you. It will also help you make the right choice about 90% of the time.

Before I wrap up this chapter, I want to share what I have found to help my spirit and what I have found that has hurt my spirit.

things that help your spirit:

Dwelling on the true, honorable, right and good. The "junk" in the world today makes it is easy to get down trodden and defeated before leaving the house in the morning. Find something good to read and dwell on, or review a good thing that has happened in your own life. Can't think of anything good? Well, you're breathing aren't you? You have a spirit within you that you can choose to use for good today. Which leads me to the second thing that helps my spirit.

Choose to do the right thing. You get to choose and make judgments everyday about what to do and how to do them, when to do them or even whether or not to do them. Choose the wise thing and it will be soothing to your soul.

Listen to and act on what you know to be true. Don't act contrary to what you believe to be true. Always be searching for the truth. Ask is it true? But, always be harmonious in your actions. If you believe something is right, act upon that, but always be testing your beliefs with the test of truth. Remember that the truth is undeniable and it is absolute.

things that hurt your spirit:

Over emphasis on the flesh and physical appetites. The flesh has its place for sure. But, an over emphasis on the flesh has caused more problems than just about anything else. Two examples of the flesh causing problems are with food and sex. Health problems and unexpected babies are the direct result of an overemphasis on feeding the desires of the flesh.

Outright disregard for what you know to be right. Christians would call that "sin". It is the doing of something that you know is wrong. Something illegal or immoral by anyone's standards. There is no question it is wrong, but you do it anyway. Obvious examples of this would be the Columbine shooting in Colorado, or the murder and rape of a young child, but it also includes stealing from a store or wasting time at work.

Going against your conscience. In the business world, we call it incongruence. It basically means doing something that you think is wrong. It may not be illegal or even immoral, but you have a conviction against doing it, so don't. When you do, you do damage to your own spirit. Examples of this might include drinking alcohol, legal gambling or smoking. None of which are inherently wrong, illegal, or immoral, but if they go against your conscious you do well to listen.

This is where life truly starts. In the spirit. It truly is a matter of life and death as well as a matter of freedom and slavery. That is why the spirit is so important.

After the spirit, the second area of life I have found that makes a profound difference is your mind. That is the topic of the next chapter.

I will share with you what I have found about where wisdom comes from, how to get it and why it is so important today. In addition, I will provide two tests you can use to tell wisdom from foolishness.

wisdom

"If you are going to win any battle, you have to do one thing. You have to make the mind run the body. Never let the body tell the mind what to do... the body is never tired if the mind is not tired."
General George Patton

"The fear of the Lord is the beginning of wisdom."
King Solomon Proverbs 9:10

Thomas Edison, Cher, Walt Disney, Richard Branson, Jay Leno, Whoopi Goldberg, Ted Turner and my hero Winston Churchill all have something in common.

Can you guess what it is?

....they were all dyslexic!

It requires a lot of reading for these people to do what they have done. Do you know how hard it is for a dyslexic person to read?

But not a single one of those great people let dyslexia keep them from being all they were created to be.

Is a lack of wisdom holding you back? If it is then go get it! If you don't think you can, think again.

Because it really speaks to the problem I think most people have in struggling for success --- **they believe** they're lacking something that, if they possessed it, would make them successful. When the truth is, they already possess everything they need, they may be small seeds, but they are seeds none-the-less. They simply must be nurtured to grow strong.

This feeling of deficiency can be directly associated to low self-respect.

There is an ancient script that says if you know what to do and don't do it you are missing the mark and it will cause great mental and emotional trauma in your life5. (One of the actions mentioned in the previous chapter that harm your spirit.)

Because you know what to do and don't, you are destroying a piece of your self-respect. I see this in my life and the life of my kids. The weekends when the work gets done first thing Saturday makes for a much more enjoyable weekend. But, the weekend when I put off the work or my kids wait until Sunday night to do their homework creates unnecessary stress.

That simple example illustrates how doing less than we could or should affects our mental state. What about putting off something like a health program or wealth program or a spiritual program?

See, these things may be pushed down out of our conscience, but in our subconscious they are still there. They are seeds, appearing to be dead, yet they will sprout seedlings of self-doubt, fear and diminished self-respect.

You can't believe one thing and act inconsistently for very long without a negative result rearing it's ugly head. Belief and actions are intimately related. You must either change your beliefs or change your actions or you will go crazy.

Wis•dom /´wiz•dem/*n* 1. the knowledge and experience needed to make sensible decisions and judgments, or the good sense shown by the decisions and judgments made

Based on this definition you can gain wisdom from knowledge and experience in order to make sensible decisions. Knowledge and experience can come from yourself or from someone else.

Some lessons are much too expensive to learn on your own. It is much better to learn them through someone else. In particular, life itself can be quite a thorough teacher, but life is also very unforgiving. Just ask the single mom, the convicted drunk driver in prison, or the desperate person living in debt.

Benjamin Franklin's story of "the Whistle" explains how the young child paid too high a price for his toy. Yes, the child did receive the whistle, but he paid too a high a price for it. I can assure you that I paid too much for many whistles and have the holes in my life to prove it. (you can download the "Whistle" article at www.getyourpoopinagroup.com/whistle)

I used to say that those experiences made me the man that I am today. No regrets.

Not anymore. That was childish thinking. It is time to put away childish thinking. True, the experiences made me who I am and I am thankful for that. But, I deeply regret certain things I have done. The debt I accumulated, the pain I have caused and the deception I used to live by slowly destroyed a part of me.

Those regrets can never be fully recovered. It is like having an arm amputated. There will always be a part of me missing. I will have to do the best I can with only one arm. But, it will not grow back. There has been permanent damage and only through God's grace have I been forgiven and am able to carry on.

No. Personal experience carries too great a cost. But, I also know that most people have enough pride and arrogance to think that they know better, especially those under 30. These are destined to repeat the same mistakes made by others.

IF, however, you have a certain desire for legitimate shortcuts may I suggest for your reading the ancient book of Proverbs found in the Bible. This is a 31 chapter book on life and wisdom written specifically to young men not yet married.

In general there is intellectual wisdom and there is practical wisdom. Intellectual wisdom can be developed and grown through a variety of sources and there can be value found in testing a lot of different beliefs and sources.

But, practical, wisdom –life lessons- on the other hand are not that forgiving. For example, research suggests that a teenager that chooses to be sexually active is three times more likely to commit suicide and six times more likely to be depressed than teenagers who are not sexually active.[10]

"...order leads to wisdom. Wisdom is the essence of man. It is that ability to discern life's patterns and those of the Word of God so that he can live life with skill."
Dr. David DeWitt - *The Mature Man, page 119*

In addition, a majority of men and women wish they would have waited longer before becoming sexually active. But, unfortunately, that is not one of those areas in which you can turn back the clock. It is like burning your hand on the stove. Once you touch the fire, you are burned for life. You can take steps to avoid getting burned again in the future, but the initial burn remains and you will always have the scar to show for it.

This is just a simple example of how life experiences can be harsh and unforgiving.

---

[10]www.getyourpoopinagroup.com/sexdepression.pdf

Wisdom affects all areas of your life and is more valuable than money, power and health. You have heard it said that "A fool and his money are soon parted." Well, it is only a matter of time before a healthy rube becomes very sick. In addition, powerful fools do more damage than weak ones.

But, if you have wisdom you can develop and cultivate the areas of money, power and health in your life.

what you know effects your earning power

A short-sighted person at 16 thinks he has all the wisdom and education he needs. He thinks, "I can get by, I hate school and I want to go make some money."

I know where he is coming from, in fact, I believe everything that he says. There is very little I learned in high school (and college for that matter) that I use on a regular daily basis. The reality is a lot of what I was taught had to be untaught to make it in life.

But, and this is a big "but", the world doesn't think that way. They will later on perhaps, but at the start, employers want to know that you can finish what you start, can be responsible enough to get decent grades, and put forth the required effort to graduate.

That is what formal education is all about.

Remember what Percy Walker was quoted as saying, *"You can get all "A's" in school and still flunk life. That does not mean however that if you get all 'C's' (or worse) you will pass life."*

Formal education is simply one test or measure that the marketplace uses to place a value on your earning power and potential.

Your earning potential or the value you bring to the marketplace is one of the biggest assets you have, especially if you are just starting out. One of the simplest and easiest ways to increase your earning power is to get the most education you can afford.

What do the stats say about education?

Education Level	Per Hour	Per Month	Per Year
Did Not Finish High School	$8.42	$1,348	$17,514
High School Graduate	$11.98	$1,916	$24,918
Some College or Associate Degree	$13.95	$2,232	$29,016
College Graduate	$20.53	$3,284	$42,702

Now, there is no reason you shouldn't get a high school diploma. It's free and society, set it up so it is easy to go to school. If you don't have your diploma, get it.

The difference between the high school graduate and the college graduate is about $1500 per month or $18,000 per year. The question you have to ask yourself is how much do you want to get paid for the hour you are working? The hour is the same no matter where you are working. It is still 60 minutes at Wal Mart or McDonalds. Whether you are the guy sweeping the floor or the manager. You will spend the hour, doing what? Earning what?

What if you can't afford college? Listen to Dave Ramsey. He has a plethora of stories of students who couldn't afford it and somehow found a way. He can be found at www.daveramsey.com.

The issue really isn't about affording it however. The real issue is whether or not you see the value in the education or not. If you see the value, you will find a way. If you get uncomfortable enough, you will find a way. I know you can.

There are many people willing to help the person who sincerely wants to grow. Remember that sincerity is proven through hard work and intelligent cooperation with how the world works.

If you choose to cheat, cut corners and get something for nothing, the world will eventually sniff you out and shut you down every time.

As a business owner, I can tell you that honest, hard-working and faithful employees are very difficult to find. When you find one, you want to do everything in your power to keep one. If there is an employee helping me make a higher profit, making things easier for me and serving customers with the owner's best interest in mind, the wise owner will do everything in his power to keep that person and pay them more and more.

I am fascinated by ball players and entertainers who make millions of dollars per year. What a great country it is when we can afford to pay people like that to perform in a way that they do. Look at Rush Limbaugh. Love him or hate him, you can't argue with a $400 million contact, with a $100 million signing bonus, just for offering conservative opinions on news and politics.

I am more fascinated by the short-sighted person who thinks that it is somehow wrong to make that much money. I am not sure why this is. Maybe it is jealousy. Maybe they think they don't deserve it. Maybe they were treated unfairly by someone with a lot of money. Who knows? Whatever the reason, they are angry about people with a lot of money.

Their argument is that it should be given to the poor instead. "Nobody needs that much money," they claim. So they attack the person, their motives and their great ability.

There is an ancient story about a group of men who traveled around following a great leader.[11] One day, a woman came up to the leader and poured very expensive perfume on the leader's feet. How expensive you ask? About a year's salary worth. You might think that to be quite a generous "waste" of money.

One of the followers of this great leader used a similar argument. He thought it was a waste of money that she poured out that expensive perfume. Instead, it should be given to the poor. To put it mildly, the leader was ticked off! He said, leave her alone! What she is doing is a great thing. You will always have the poor with you, but you will not always have me.

He went on to say that he knew the motives of the person criticizing the woman. He wanted the money for himself (i.e. jealousy and greed).

[11]John 12:1-7

How a person earns their money, gives their money and spends their money is their own business. Profit, hope, value are all very good things. Profit is making something out of nothing or improving the value of something. Making something better than how they found it.

If a person can make $300 million dollars playing a sport then that is wonderful. Why in the world would someone be willing to pay a ball player that much? Because he is worth it to the marketplace. It doesn't mean that he is valuable to his wife, kids or community. Maybe he is, maybe he isn't. But, if that ball player can help a team owner win games, sell tickets and create more than $300 million in profits, then it is a good deal to the owner. Why shouldn't he pay him that much?

The question is how valuable are you to the marketplace? The marketplace is where you sell your value in exchange for an agreed upon rate.

You want more money per hour, then bring more value to the marketplace. People will pay big bucks for big value - always have and always will. The wise understand this.

health connection to education & wisdom

Educated people live longer and are healthier than their foolish and uneducated counterparts. How can you even place a value on a longer and healthier life? What would one more healthy year of life be worth to you?

Don't fall victim to the lie that all the elderly are sickly and just waiting around to die in a worthless pitiful state. Far from it. An overwhelming majority of seniors live healthy, self determined lives not relying on anything thing or anyone else. They are not dependent on the government and they are not a drain on their families. The opposite is actually true.

A full 80% are healthy and doing well. 80%!

A recent Newsweek article reported that people with some college courses, (they didn't even need to graduate mind you), experienced longer and healthier life than those who did not.

So, improving your mind with wisdom not only has a positive financial impact on your life, but it also contributes to a long and healthier life itself.

Maybe that's why one of the richest men who ever lived said that wisdom is so important. The ancient story goes something like this:

God came down in a dream and said, "You are the new king, so I will grant you whatever your heart desires."

The young man was concerned about how he would rule the nation and so he asked for a heart of wisdom in which to judge and rule this great people. He wanted to be able to discern good from evil.

God was so pleased by his response that he gave the young man not only wisdom but also riches and honor as well.

We all know that education is not the same as wisdom and that there are different kinds of education and wisdom. For example, you can have mechanical wisdom or creative wisdom, literary wisdom or mathematical wisdom, athletic wisdom or emotional wisdom. We all have some kind of blend of each of them.[12]

wisdom is sexy

What about sex? How does wisdom help in that area?

Well, a wise person takes a look at the available options and uses his good judgment to discern good from bad, profit from loss, and chooses accordingly. A wise person looks at the available resources and can make up his own mind.

There is a lot of distraction however making it difficult to see the truth. A fool gets lured in by a bat of an eyelash or a particular "look" or "wiggle". The wise man looks past the distraction and looks at the heart. That is no simple matter either!

When I was growing up, when the earth was still cooling, (you know a long time ago, before cable tv), we used to have these "Rabbit Ears" on top of

---

[12]The various gifts of wisdom is explained in detail in the book "Emotional Intelligence" by Daniel Goleman

the tv to try and get good reception. Typically, you would change the channel and have to adjust the antenna to see the picture clearly. The station always put out the signal, but you couldn't "get it" unless you adjusted your antenna to receive the signal.

There is so much static out there today that it can be hard to dial in to the truth, but it is out there and it has always been sending it's signal. In fact, it has been shouting from the roof top but the naïve and the simple have a hard time adjusting the rabbit ears to see and hear it. Especially when much of culture is saying that truth doesn't even exist.

If you fail to understand that there is absolute truth and that it can be known, you will be prey to the idea of someone else's definition of "truth". Their "truth" will enslave you.

Here are some simple facts about sex (expanded more in the marriage chapter): Married people report having more sex than their unmarried and divorced contemporaries. So, if you want to have the most sex, getting married is the wisest choice.

What about the quality you ask?

I'm glad you did.

Married couples also have the highest level of both physical and emotional satisfaction compared to any other group measured. That's right, **the highest level** reported of any group.

So, if you are interested in having the best sex and having it more often, the wise choice is to get married and stay married.

a closer look at fools

Unfortunately, we have become so preoccupied with "self-esteem" and feeling good about ourselves that we are willing to forego a blessing if we are not made to feel good.

For example,

A rube says, "I don't want to go unless you want me and make me feel good about myself."

The wise say, "I don't care whether you want me or how you make me feel. I am sticking around you for what I can learn from you."

Look at any great coach. They push and challenge and push again to make those athletes be as good as they can be. Their job is not to make them feel good, but to make them better players to win games. To the degree that the athlete sees value in what the coach is doing, he will "buy in" to the program. To use a poker term, they have gone "all in" because they see value in it. If the coach is overly concerned about what the player thinks about them and their self esteem, the coach ceases to be coach and growth is thwarted.

It is like allowing a teenager to mess his pants and say, "Oh, that's OK, and let him sit in it so he doesn't have to feel bad about himself." No. You correct them, let them clean up their mess and teach them a better way to live than sitting in their own excrement.

I know that takes judgment and truth and seems awfully intolerant. But, the fact is, that is what true love requires.

who are the fools?

Fools say in their heart that there is no God.

It is hard to find a lot of professing atheists these days. At one time, they abounded in the US. There is a lot of distraction and confusion about who God is and what He has done and is doing. Where to find Him? Etc. But, the fool has said that there is no God.

Fools say that you shouldn't judge but you should be tolerant.

The greatest "virtue" in today's world seems to be tolerance. The world says, "Don't judge between right and wrong and have an open mind." The wise know how foolish that statement is. The world today says that the search is everything and discovery matters little. This view quickly proves unsatisfactory. An open mind can be an empty head and tolerance can be indistinguishable from believing nothing.

Fools don't like feedback

A telltale sign of a fool is how they respond to feedback. A fool will hate you if you give feedback, whereas the wise will love you for it.

For example, you see a man with a booger on his face and you tell him about it. He says, "Why don't you mind your own business? You don't know what you are talking about. Don't judge me!"

I know it is a silly example and no one would truly respond that way if they did have a meat patty hanging off the side of their face, or their fly open for that matter. But, how often do we see an enemy created when the truth is told?[13]

An ancient leader wrote a letter to some of his early students and asked them, "Have I now become your enemy by telling you the truth?"

They were acting foolishly.

Fools place a higher value on the Earth and the environment than on people and God.

An ancient writing says that the people in their great wisdom began to worship created things rather than the creator. This did not sit well with the creator who declared that "Thinking they were wise they became fools, they became futile in their speculations, and their foolish heart was darkened."[14]

who are the wise?

A wise man does not boast in his wisdom, or his might, or his riches.

A wise man is humble. A humble man is secure. Only the secure can be humble. A secure man places his value and life on something greater than wisdom, money and power. That is what makes him wise.

One of my all time favorite movies is "Braveheart" starring Mel Gibson as William Wallace. When William was a young boy he was fascinated by the strength and power found in the sword of his uncle. Knowing his fascination

[13]Galatians 4:16
[14]Romans 1:1-20

with the sword, the uncle tapped young William on the head and said, "First, learn to use this (pointing to his head). Then I'll teach you to use this (pointing to the sword)."

The wise keep on growing.

The wise keep increasing in wisdom and stature both among God and among men. A wise man examines himself and tests himself. He holds himself accountable and has other people help him as well. He is always learning and growing. He knows his strengths and weaknesses and acts accordingly.

The wise test and examine everything for truth.

When the Christian belief was just starting to take root, one of the early leaders was a man by the name of Paul. He was teaching some new material to the people. He encouraged them to test it, examine it. He said examine everything carefully; hold fast to that which is good. Paul called those who "tested, judged and discerned" to be of "more noble mind" than the others.

The wise know that there is a time for everything under the sun. A time to laugh and to cry, to fight and to make peace, to live and to die. The wise are able to discern the time in which each of these is necessary. The fool does not discern these things. Therefore, the fool will make peace when he should fight, laugh when he should cry and die when he should live.

The wise are hard working and morally pure.

Hard work along with moral excellence leads to knowledge. Immorality is the single biggest detriment to wisdom and truth. A wise man's heart directs him toward the right path, but the foolish man's heart directs him toward the wrong path. Turning away from evil is what personifies the wise man. They flee immorality. Flee, like run, as in a Gazelle fleeing from a Lion.

How does one become wise?

Know where to find it.

The first step to getting anything is to know where to look for it. For the Believer, wisdom comes from God.

Ask for it.

That is what the great king did earlier in this chapter. He was given a choice of anything and he chose wisdom. If you choose it and faithfully ask for it you will receive it.

It starts with fear.

Fear of the one giving wisdom is what starts the wisdom process. It is sort of like a fire. Fire is a powerful and fearful thing if it is not taken seriously. Used correctly, it can warm, cook and purify. As soon as the fear of fire is gone it will burn and destroy.

There is some fuzzy thinking with regard to fear nowadays. People ask me, "Do you really mean fear as in 'terror' or do you mean fear as in 'respect'?"

"I mean fear as in terror."

"That doesn't sound like the loving God I know," is the typical response.

"I know. That's because we don't talk much about fear these days. But, remember it was the loving Jesus who said to fear God because of what he can do."[15]

"But, let me ask you something. If fear is to be defined as 'respect' like for a grandfather, as you suggest, who gets to determine what 'respect' looks like? You or the one being respected?"

"You get to determine what respect looks like."

Respect is something that is defined by you and given on your own terms. You get to decide, you are in control, you are god. The attitude of fear, like in our fire example however, puts the proper perspective on the relationship. The one in charge is the one to be feared. Respect warps that view and changes the student to a teacher. In essence, with 'respect' I get to become my own God and set my own rules. I get the choice.

It may seem a bit difficult to swallow, but nothing of real value comes without a cost or comes very easy. Wisdom is like that. It starts slowly, then

[15]Mathew 10:28, Luke 12:5, Hebrews 10:31

like an investment earning compound interest in the bank it will grow and grow. It is a very good thing to acquire.

Wisdom is another good thing to bet on.

Here are some other ideas to help with regard to wisdom:

Public Speaking: People who speak well in public are perceived to be more intelligent than those who don't.

Be Quiet: Even a fool who keeps his mouth shut is considered wise. Why open your mouth and remove any doubt? ?

Increase Your Vocabulary: People with a better handle of the English language and those who have improved their use of vocabulary words are viewed as more wise and intelligent than others.

Read! One of the best ways to increase knowledge and wisdom is to turn off the computer and TV and read. The Book of Proverbs in the Bible was written by the wisest man ever to live. It is broken into 31 chapters and can easily be read one chapter each day for a month. Continue that for a year and watch what happens.

health

"Of course your life is more than your body, but the body is one of the first gifts given to us by God. How we take care of body is a reflection of how we view that gift as well as a reflection on how we view ourselves."

"The spirit is willing but, the body is weak."
Jesus, Matthew 26:41

Your health is probably the single most valuable asset that you presently have. Any young man can enter the work world and immediately earn a living. A healthy young man that can burn the midnight oil, give more because he does not fatigue easily, is always on time and available because he never gets sick, is a real asset to a company seeking to compete in the world arena.

So, what are the half dozen keys to good health?

Diet, exercise, attitude, friends, image and integrity.

There have been literally thousands of books, tapes and seminars designed and developed for diet.

Here are some common sense ideas for you to ponder. Most of us were born fairly healthy. We were somewhat active in school through recess and phys-ed. But then, through neglect, a majority of Americans stop exercising and start eating.

There are many ways to determine your "ideal weight" but for simplicity (remember the 80/20 rule) let's use the BMI chart that follows. Simply find your height on the left side of the scale and match it up with your current weight on the top. Where these two points intersect is what your current "BMI" or "Body Mass Index" is. This is a good guideline for where you should be to be considered healthy in terms of your weight.

Weight in Pounds

Height	120	130	140	150	160	170	180	190	200	210	220	230	240	250
4'6"	29	31	34	36	39	41	43	46	48	51	53	56	58	60
4'8"	27	29	31	34	36	38	40	43	45	47	49	52	54	56
4'10"	25	27	29	31	34	36	38	40	42	44	46	48	50	52
5'0"	23	25	27	29	31	33	35	37	39	41	43	45	47	49
5'2"	22	24	26	27	29	31	33	35	37	38	40	42	44	46
5'4"	21	22	24	26	28	29	31	33	34	36	38	40	41	43
5'6"	19	21	23	24	26	27	29	31	32	34	36	37	39	40
5'8"	18	20	21	23	24	26	27	29	30	32	34	35	37	38
5'10"	17	19	20	22	23	24	26	27	29	30	32	33	35	36
6'0"	16	18	19	20	22	23	24	26	27	28	30	31	33	34
6'2"	15	17	18	19	21	22	23	24	26	27	28	30	31	32
6'4"	15	16	17	18	20	21	22	23	24	26	27	28	29	30
6'6"	14	15	16	17	19	20	21	22	23	24	25	27	28	29
6'8"	13	14	15	17	18	19	20	21	22	23	24	25	26	28

Height in Feet and Inches

Underweight   Healthy Weight   Overweight   Obese

In addition to the BMI it is good to look at what you weighed at 18 as a good indication of what your ideal weight should be. Most people over 30 will give you a number within 10 pounds of what would be their healthiest weight. Even the people who were overweight at 18 would give their eye-teeth to weigh what they did at 18 again.

Why 18? Because most people do not grow taller after eighteen so they don't add more bone and very few add more muscle. So, that leaves fat, which you don't need.

So between the BMI and your weight at eighteen you have a pretty good idea of where you should be.

The reason why this is so important now is it is much easier to stay in shape than to get into shape. If you are close to age eighteen now, it is easier to maintain that weight than to try and lose a bunch later on.

You may not feel successful or healthy and see much room for improvement, but don't sell yourself short. At eighteen you will be about as healthy as you are going to ever be unless you take steps to defend against the downward pull of aging.

I like to use the airplane example. It takes a lot of energy to get that big 747 off the ground. No, I am not calling you a "jumbo jet" that must get off the couch.

The point is that it takes a lot of energy and fuel to get that baby up in the air. But, once it is up there the amount of fuel and energy needed to maintain it is a fraction of what it took to get it up.

At 18, you are already up there. Gravity is always wanting to pull you down. The gravity is food, insufficient rest, alcohol, drugs, tobacco, TV and video games etc. You know what they are.

Ask any smoker: it is much easier to never start than to quit. The same holds true for the alcoholic.

My tendancy is to be weak and lazy. I want to do the very minimum I can to get the results I must have. I have found that it is easier to defeat small enemies than large enemies. It is easier to lose 10 pounds than to lose 50.

I weighed 155 pounds at eighteen. I got up to 203 my peak 10 years later. I can tell you, it took radical action to get back down.

The best thing I did was to put on a bathing suit and start taking photos. That was the kick in the pants that I needed. Disgust is an amazing motivator!

It took only 84 days of commitment and I was on a roll. I got involved with the "Body For Life" competition with my wife and we did it together. When people have a common goal and can encourage one another to succeed it can be a wonderful thing.

There are many, many programs out there to help. The key is to find one that puts the odds of success in your favor.

How you do this is through accountability, a clear focused goal, and most importantly a picture of the old and a picture of the new.

Why do this?

Healthy bodies lead to healthy minds and less depression.

Many people don't do well because they don't feel well.

You can work harder, longer.

You will have energy for family and friends.

You will also have better sex (improve heart and blood flow to organs)

Exercise helps to manage stress and anxiety.

Let's face it. In the real world people judge you on how you look. They believe that an outward appearance is simply a reflection of an inward belief and mindset. People see an out-of-shape and unhealthy person and they make judgments about who you are and the type of person you are.

I am not talking about a warped view that we all must look like super models. Instead, I encourage a basic common sense approach to life.

Healthy looking people are generally healthy. Most people are out of shape because of the choices they have made and a belief system that allows them to think that it is ok.

The following are the basics:

| exercise | diet | friends |
| attitude | integrity | image |

attitude

Health and attitude play an interesting and intimate role with each other. It is also related to work.

Often times, I do not feel like working out and I have to "trick" myself into it. I'll put on work out gear or drive to the athletic club, or just say I will commit to 10 minutes and then stop if I don't feel like it.

Nine times out of ten once I start moving I feel like finishing. I may not always work, but I typically feel better (i.e. improved attitude) just by starting even though I don't feel like it.

The thing is that after I have worked out and eaten well for a while, I tend to get into a groove and don't want to miss a day. So, I force myself with discipline to get through the initial inertia, and then once I get going, a new habit helps me keep going.

Of course there are times when I feel like not working out. But once the habit has been created and I begin to feel and look better, it always makes me do better. That encourages me to keep going.

It is a classic Chicken and egg scenario. Which came first, the attitude or the health? Health or the attitude? Who knows? The bottom line is that they are closely related to each other. You can spend a lot of time thinkng about it, or you can get off the couch and get moving. You don't need all the answers to know how this works; just understand that it does and get moving.

You can study how the tree makes fruit or you can go out and pick some. I suggest picking the fruit and let someone else figure out how it works. I am more interested in the results.

Attitude affects your health in another profound way. Studies have proven that a positive and optimistic outlook on things keeps you looking younger, but also minimizes your health risks.

Happy people are sick less often and have more energy in general. This makes sense. If you are living your life on purpose, have a positive outlook and are working toward a meaningful goal that you are confident you can achieve, you will feel great.

"Optimism is more important than education, intelligence, experience, family or national origin."
Dr, Martin Seligman

Compare this to a person stuck in a rut, without hope in the future and with debt in the mail. What is the point? Like Cameron from the movie "Ferris Buelers' Day Off". He feels better when he is sick.

In addition, there is a real physical and chemical connection to health and attitude. As I runner I know this all too well.

The endorphins, neoprenephrine and melatonin that are created and secreted into the blood stream as a result of working out are the same chemicals that are triggered when a person does certain drugs. There is a very real result from the drugs (just like there is a real result from working out).

The problem with the drugs however, is that once you start taking them, your body loses its ability to create the "feel good" chemicals on their own.

Do you want the "pay now play later" philosophy of an athlete or the "play now, pay later" philosophy of an addict? One will lead to freedom, profit and joy. The other will lead to slavery, loss, and bitterness.

friends

Loners tend to be very unhappy people. Unhappy people tend to be self centered and bitter. Bitterness leads to a sour outlook and a sour face and poor health.

I am not talking about being the life of the party. Just one good friend is all it takes. Two can be better. Two offers a much better return on the investment.

Studies show that if one person working alone can build 10 widgets, two people working together can do 24. 1 plus 1 should equal 2 but it doesn't. Why not? Not sure. You can study why this is, or you can just apply it and make it work for you.

Three people is even better than two. Instead of 1 + 1 + 1 = 3. It adds up to 4. Ancient wisdom states that the reason for this is that when you stumble alone, it is difficult if not impossible to get up. A friend on the other hand can help you back up, or keep you from falling in the first place (through encouragement).[16]

integrity

People all across the world see the value in integrity. People like to do business with those whom they can trust.

Telling the truth, the whole truth and nothing but the truth is a great shortcut to success. Despite what the media says, did you know that companies that have "the golden rule" (or something to that effect) in their corporate mission statement earn an average of 45% more per year than those who don't?

Enron, once was considered the largest bankruptcy of all time. Now in 2008 it is the investment banks who are in trouble as a result of the Fannie Mae and Freddie Mac mortgage abuse. These failures resulted in hundreds of billions of dollars lost, not only for corporate America but also for senior citizens who worked years to save the money. The senior citizens invested in stocks and mutual funds only to see a large portion of it disappear one day due to the unethical behavior by it's executives.

Such behavior leads to the perception that all businesses are run by crooks and criminals. Or that "profit is evil" etc. The reality is, 98% of all businesses are run by the most ethical and intelligent people in the world. If they were not run by ethical people, they would not be as successful.

[16]Ecclesiastes 4:9-12

The thing about integrity is that there are the obvious ramifications of telling the truth. For example, you may need to clean up a mess you made or you may need to right a wrong that you did..

But, if you start telling lies, then you have to start remembering to cover your tracks, including remembering whom you told what and to whom. Talk about a web of confusion and mental anguish. No wonder liars get sick!

The other part of integrity is a little more subtle but can be much more damaging. That is the integrity within you. Be true to who you are.

I know this can be extremely difficult for a number of reasons. You may not be sure what you want yet, so you flounder in an area. You may want to please a parent, a friend or a church youth group.

For whatever strange reason I looked forward to turning 40 years old. Perhaps that came from the numerous stories I read about people who claimed that they truly started to "live" when they turned 40.

Why you might ask? They say that when you turn 40 you quit worrying so much about what other people think and begin to follow that inner passion and desire that you have been hiding under a rock for so many years.

Oprah Winfrey said that when she turned 40 something inside her started to let loose. I have an idea of what she means. I worked at a bank, sold stocks, worked in manufacturing and had my own company all by the age of 40. But, it wasn't until I started writing and speaking about what I am passionate about that I started feeling that I was truly being true to myself and began to use what God had planted deep inside me.

There is definitely a confidence that naturally occurs the older you get. You have seen a lot of life and realize that you are mortal. Mortality is something that most people under 25 haven't realized yet.

For good reason I might add. When you are younger you see 40 as a long way off and 80, well that's another lifetime away. You have plenty of time to make changes, make money, do the deal, kiss the girl etc.

It is like the day before Christmas compared to thinking about Christmas in July. There is a heightened awareness and anticipation when the date approaches. There is a sense of urgency that is created. You just don't have that urgency or awareness at 20 like you do at 40.

I think that is why they call it a "mid life crisis". By the way, for a great local Grand Rapids, MI band see mlc.com. These are some local men that kept their dream alive and have a great local band in order to help them through their own mid-life crisis.

So, follow your heart. Do what you love and things will happen.

Many, many people go to their grave with their music still left in them. Now, granted some music is probably best left where it is and doesn't need to come out. Things like immorality and the dark side of man are best left alone, (even better if you aggressively destroy those weeds in your garden). But, that is not what I am talking about. Rather, I am talking about the courage and faith to step out and grow. Living timid and small doesn't help anyone anyway. Take the risk, make the call and go for it!

The reality is that if you do not stay true to yourself and live consistently with what you believe to be true, you will be miserable. You can run and stay ahead of it for awhile, but eventually you will begin to slow down and what is inside will start to rear it's head and want to come out.

You don't have to wait until 40 to start either. Do it when you are young. Travel the world. Work at the dude ranch (Lost Valley Ranch in Colorado is awesome by the way). Join the Marines, heck even join the circus.

Image: How you see yourself is the final piece of the puzzle. Although, I listed it here at the end, it is actually the first thing that must change before you can have lasting good health.

If you see yourself as sick and unhealthy that is exactly what you will be. The picture and image you hold of yourself must be changed to a realistic and heavenly picture of true health.

Too many mis-beliefs about health are holding people back. The Matthew McConaughey look for men or the Kate Hudson look for women are two examples. Those are special people indeed, but that is not you.

Do your best with what God gave you. You may not look like the models you see on the magazine racks or perform on the athletic field like the "all star", but, that does not mean that it is OK to "let yourself go" physically or not do your best in the competitive arena.

It is like the guy that has a tire blow out on his way to work. Instead of getting out of the car and fixing the flat, he says, "Well, since the one tire is blown, I might as well blow out the rest of them."

NO! Don't think like the Rube!

We can see how silly that would be, yet we do it day in and day out if we are not careful.

Get a better image of yourself. (May I suggest the image God has of you as defined in the Bible?) You are worth it and you can do it. Many others before you have.

The other part of image to consider is how you feel about yourself. Doing less than you can has a subtle way of eating away at your self respect. Often times, low self respect reveals itself in an unhealthy maintenance of the body. It is simply a manifestation of not caring. Your self-respect must be guarded tenaciously.

Whenever you do less than you could, or do something that you believe to be wrong, you eat away at your self-respect.

Self-respect is something that is earned through effort, integrity and each small victory.

You know when you do not put in the effort. You can fool your boss, fool your teacher, and even your spouse. But, you can never fool yourself. You know when you did your best and when you didn't. Remember, you will reap what you sow, not to think so is naïve.

basics

> Diet plan: "Eat real food more often."
> Save the "easy $39.95 monthly payments"
> and pay off debt instead.

Diet: eat more fresh fruits and vegetables and avoid the poisons of smoking, drugs and alcohol.

Exercise: get moving with some aerobic type activity like walking, biking or swimming along with some strength training like push ups, sit ups and pull ups.

Friends: be careful who you allow to get too close to you and be aware of what they are planting in your brain. Toxic people are just as hazardous (if not more so) to your health as toxic things you put into your body.

Attitude: by dwelling on the good, the pure, the true and the honorable you will nurture positive attributes that will result in a healthier body. A positive attitude has a greater effect on your body's health than diet and exercise. So, don't let bitterness overtake you in the midst of disappointment. For that little root of bitterness will grow and cause you to become less than you are. Smile, it will improve your face value!

Integrity: the truth will set you free. Facing the reality of where you are will begin the breaking chains, allowing you to truly be free. Any deceit and lying will wreak havoc on your soul and be a stumbling block to good health.

Image: change the picture you have of yourself. This will require a little effort and faith in the beginning but, as the picture is held in your mind and the new activities begin to take root, you will see changes in your life that will last.

Get smart! Even a little college has a very positive effect on your health and life expectancy. (Newsweek article)

Wisdom says, "I will buffet my body and make it my slave." The fool says, "I will let my body rule my thoughts and actions."

A wise person understands that beauty is vain, but a woman who fears the Lord is valuable indeed. No matter how well you take care of your body and how good you look, you are fighting a losing battle. Eventually, you will die. The body is in a constant state of decline. However, you can continue to renew your mind and spirit until the day you die.

The fool says, "What's the point? I am going to die anyway. When you're number's up, you're number's up. Live it up and party!"

These foolish notions only short circuit your effectiveness and the stewardship of your body. You give your car a tune up, change the oil from time to time, wash it and put gas in it, so why not do the same with your body? This isn't about worshipping your body; rather, it is about taking very good care of an extremely valuable gift that has been giving to you.

Did you know about the connection that love & intimacy has on health?

In his book, Love & Survival, Dr. Dean Ornish points out that love and intimacy are more powerful determinants of health than improved diet, stopping smoking, genetic make-up, more exercise, or prescription drugs. Research suggests that oxytocin is behind these gains If companionship came in drug form, doctors who failed to prescribe it would be guilty of malpractice. (Ornish, 1998).

Take a look at the following common sense approach to exercise?

Aerobic exercise, like running, swimming, biking etc., all work to increase your heart rate while working out. The result of this increased effort is that your resting heart rate is lower, resulting in a heart that is more efficient and beats fewer times to produce the same amount of blood flow.

The following illustrates this:

Heart beats per day comparison:

Non-Runners

Minutes per day	Heart Rate	TTL Beats per day
1440	80	115200

Runners

Minutes per day	Heart Rate	TTL Beats per day	
60	180	10800	Running
1380	60	82800	Not Running
		93600	**TTL Beats**

Comparison of daily heartbeats

Runners	Non-Runners	Beats Saved
115200	93600	-21600

This is a 19% savings in heartbeats each day!

So, let's just say that God gave you so many heartbeats until you were going to die. Kind of like the warranty on your car. The thing always seems to break right after the warranty expires.

If we each get 1,000,000 beats, the person who exercises will use those heart beats in 10 days where the non-exerciser will use them in 8. So, every 10 days the non-exerciser is gives up two. The bottom line is that the exerciser will get an extra 15 years of life compared to the non-exerciser. 15 years! That is what happens with lowering your heart rate.

Can you imagine what will be the result if you eat a little better and keep your attitude in check? The results are probably around an additional 25 years on the average life span. For a man the life expectancy is 72, that will put him at 97.

quality vs. quantity?

Who wants to live that long you say? Everybody it seems! Observation shows that people pay a lot of money to stick around as long as possible. A majority of health care dollars are spent at the end of one's life trying to maintain health or prolong one's life. By taking care of your equipment earlier in life you can help maintain it and prolong it for many, many years. It is very similar to saving and investing money. Starting early with small amounts leads to huge gains in the future. The sooner you start the better (more on that in the money chapter).

Remember Winston Chruchill didn't become a man of prominence and leadership until he was over 70 years old. Ronald Reagan, the president of the United States credited with destroying the evil empire of the Soviet Union, was 70 years old when he took office. He was 78 when he finished up his second term.

Don't pooh, pooh the notion that getting older is a bad deal. Quite the contrary. Most senior citizens are healthy and active and are not relying on anyone else for their support. They are independent and doing fine. The only thing that they truly complain about is not being used. They have so much unused capacity it boggles the mind!

Health nut, Mike Bragg died at 93 years old. He drowned while surfing off the coast of California. Dr. Norman W, Walker worked hard until the day he died when he went in to take his routine afternoon nap and never woke up, he was 99. There are countless cases of men and women like this who took steps to swing the odds in their favor for good health and vitality. It is a good bet to make!

Just don't make your body your God and worship it. Taking very good care of something is not the same as worshipping it. Remember, God judges the heart whereas man judges what you look like. You may not think that very fair, but that's the way it is.

In the next chapter I will share with you
- The best way to get ahead at work.
- How much work should you do.
- Thinking like an owner
- Do more than you get paid for.

work

"Don't waste life in doubts and fears; spend yourself on the work before you, well assured that the right performance of this hour's duties will be the best preparation for the hours and ages that will follow it."
Ralph Waldo Emerson

"Faith (belief) without work is dead."
James 2:26

It has been said that the only place where success comes before work is in the dictionary. While that may be cliché it goes without saying that hard and smart work will do more to get you ahead than just about anything else.

So, what are the half dozen keys to work?

How much, how long, think like the owner, do more than you get paid for, be faithful, develop your skills.

First things first.

how much work should you do?

That question can easily be answered by asking another question: How much money do you want to make?

The more you work the more you will probably make.

CEO's typically work 60 hours per week and watch 1 hour of television each week. The production worker typically works 40 hours per week and watches 4-6 hours of television per night.

The obvious answer however is to work as much as you can.

Assuming you start working at age 20 and stay at it for 40 years earning $30,000 you will earn well over $1.2 million in your lifetime. That is assuming no raises or enhancement of skills to become more valuable in the market-place.

how long should you work?

Retirement is basically a new concept that came into existence during the 1920's with the German Chancelor.

He found that most of his opponents were wealthy businessman. So, what did the chancellor do? He instituted a mandatory retirement for people aged 65 and older, thereby eliminating his rivals.

Retirement can't even be found in ancient texts like the Bible. In fact, it is nowhere to be found. You should work until you can't anymore.

Here's an idea. If you are over 65 years old and want to keep working, you can as long as you are still performing well. To encourage older and wiser people to stay in the work force, how about offering that all income earned by those over 65 be tax free? No taxes whatsoever for retirees who continue to work. That also means no payroll taxes for the businessman who hires them.

Wow, I wonder what that would do to the Social Security program? Think there would be any takers to that idea? I bet you there would.

But, I digress.

The reason why it is important to work forever is what retirement does to people. Not what it does for them, what it does to them. Many die a very short period after they retire. These are very capable and wise men, they have lost their purpose for living. As a consequence, they check out far too soon.

think like the owner

As a business owner I can tell you that you have no idea the amount of pressure and stress that owners have subjected themeselves too. Between taxes, employees, customers and payroll you get very little reward.

It never ends and you can never "go home". Work is always on your mind 24/7.

One of the great joys is having people working with you that knows how a business works and that if there is no profit, there is no business. If there is no business there is no job security. Job security is a result of profits; it always has been and always will be. If you truly want job security, do everything you can to help the business become even more profitable, now and in the future.

So, if an employee helps the business become more and more profitable through increased efficiency, effectiveness, creativity and personal development, the company will grow. Typically, a company will only grow to the degree that the people inside the business grow.

The employees that I get rid of fast (not fast enough in most cases, unfortunately) are the ones that have their own short-term interests at heart. I am getting better at sniffing them out, but they are a cancer in any organization.

I live in Michigan and we currently have the worst economy in the country. Why, you ask? Well, there are many reasons to be sure, but the bottom line is that business owners see Michigan as a bad place to do business. They don't think they will be as profitable in Michigan as they will be in other states.

I hear people blame the taxes, the unions, the regulations or the red tape. They may all be right. I don't know. It is easy to point fingers and say who is to blame. But to fix it, you must make it more attractive to do business here than anywhere else.

If a store wants to increase its traffic and business in its store, it holds a sale. If a girl is looking to get the attention of a young man, she will do want she can to become more attractive. If a state wants an economy to grow, it must become more attractive to business owners.

Employees are no different. I want the most attractive employees available. By "attractive" I mean are the ones that help me earn the most profit. If you have my best interest at heart through your performance, we can work well together.

The problem is that most employees see me as "the man" or "the establishment" making me the problem in this country, not the solution. They believe I don't deserve what I have; I am criminal, greedy, selfish, etc. etc. etc.

This belief (misbelief) encourages them to take from me by wasting time and attempting whatever schemes they think they can get away with. They think I am "sticking it to others", so they "stick it to me".

How far do you think that employee will get in any job? What kind of reference will they get when they go looking for another job?

One time a guy told me that they don't pay that much where he works, so he was not going to give that much. Well, I guess that's one way of looking at things. Again I ask, how far do you think that guy will go with that kind of attitude?

Still another says, I won't work that hard for another, but if I had my own business I would work my tail off. The problem with that philosophy is twofold. First, he is already working for himself and doesn't even realize it. Second, there is an ancient text that states that yif you have not been faithful with another's, who will give you that of your own.[17]

Anyone in leadership knows that you cannot be a great leader until you know how to be a great follower. More on this point in a minute.

[17]Luke 16:12

do more than you get paid for

Employees in Michigan all the time tell me through no fault of their own they got laid off. They did a great job, yet the company closed up and then stuck without a job.

I truly do empathize with these folks. It is a devastating thing to go through. Especially for a man. A man's identity is tied so closely to what he does it can drive a man to the pit of depression and despair, even suicidal. He feels like a failure and nothing else matters. It can be borderline insanity. What a man would never consider doing while gainfully employed, he will consider when he desperately needs to help his family or himself.

That being said, I can't tell you how many people have come in applying for work that didn't do a thing for the past six months because they had unemployment coming in. It wasn't until the unemployment ran out that they got serious about looking for work.

Let's say that I had an employee who was doing everything she could to help my business succeed only to have the business go under. If she were truly that valuable to me, don't you think I would find something that she could do for me? Wouldn't it be infinitely better for me to find some way for her to work with me somewhere else? If the Cleveland Cavaliers fold up their basketball franchise, do you think that LeBron James will be able to find another job for any other basketball team?

The marketplace will pay for performance. You know what? Business owners talk to each other. I know many other owners and if I have an employee that I think is top notch, I will pass their name along. I know it will come back to help me again. My friend will be in my debt for referring such a great employee to him.

The opposite is also true.

Once again it is all about profit or gain. You help me by giving more than you get paid for and your reward will be raises, better jobs, and job security. Each of us is looking out for each other through our mutual self-interest.

Yes, profit, hope, gain, are all good motivations for living.

We all do things for gain and what we perceive to be of value and in our best interest. That is called hope.

be faithful

Throw your heart into your job. Give it your all. In fact, work like you were working for God. The Bible even teaches that.[18]

Yeah, I know, the person you work for already thinks that they are God and you don't need to encourage that attitude. Well, do it anyway and you will get ahead far faster than if you don't.

I had an employee (older and wiser than I) who told me a story about when he was in the Army. His strategy was to do everything in his power to make his superior look good. It was a purely self-seeking motive too.

He rationalized (correctly, I might add) that if his superior got promoted one of two things was likely to happen. First, if the boss got promoted there was a good chance that he would take over, and if that didn't happen, there was a good chance that the superior would want to move him up along with him. He said that without fail it worked.

The best secretaries in the world know this as well. High-powered executives place an extremely high value on trust and competence. When they find a competent, capable and trustworthy executive assistant, that person soars right along with the executive.

develop your skills

The story goes that the wood-cutter can cut 35% more wood with a sharp saw than one with a dull blade.

Sharpening the saw is not the same as putting it down however. Sure, a break is a good idea when you are tired. But, that doesn't sharpen anything.

Sharpening takes additional work. The woodcutter places the blade against a grindstone to hone the edge to a razor point. In business, that

[18]Whatever you do, do your work heartily, as for the Lord rather than for men, knowing that from the Lord you will receive the reward of the inheritance. It is the Lord Christ whom you serve. Colossians 3:23-24

could be a weekend seminar or a good book that addresses a new skill. A new diet and exercise program to help you with stamina and effort at work and home. Even an inspiring story or movie can help to renew and invigorate.

One of the best skills to work at developing has to do with working with and getting along with other people. In fact, that is the #1 issue that people who hire people look for in candidates: The ability to work with and get along with other people.

Don't fall into the misconception that working at the same job for 10 years gives you 10-years of experience. If nothing else changed and you weren't proactive in your job, you most likely have 1-year of experience repeated 10 times.

It takes a conscious choice to develop valuable and marketable skills. Don't expect your boss or your spouse to do that for you either. That is something that you must take control of and intelligently spend time on yourself.

what about pay?

My liberal friends suggest that the minimum wage is far too low. They believe no one can survive at the current minmum wage levels. But, bumping it $1 or $2 wont make that much of difference either. In fact, I suggest that they bump the minimum wage to $50,000 per year or more. That way at least people can afford to live a standard of living that they would like. In fact, while were at it, why not increase it to $100,000 and then we will all be "livin' large"?

It's ludicrous I know. If the minimum wage were a ceiling then that might be a good idea, but the minimum wage is a floor not a ceiling. It is a ladder not a bed. You don't have to stay at the minimum level except by choice. The minimum wage is like the bottom rung on a ladder that you must climb and exert effort to get ahead. It is not an escalator that automatically goes up without adding additional skills or effort.

Organized labor tried to create that "escalator" system through demand. Through influence and strikes they succeeded in getting more money for the employees. For a while. Those additional costs to businesses, without the commensurate productivity and profitability gains eroded the profitability of the companies. Business owners found that competition was really hurting them, so they began looking for alternatives. Michigan is now a classic example of how that philosophy destroys the very people it tries to help.

You cannot get rich by demand, only through service. If you want to earn more for the hour you give the company then work to become more valuable to the company through skills and service.

If you get paid $10 for each hour that you work and you are responsible for generating $20 in profit for each of those hours, you have the ultimate in job security. In fact, it probably won't be long until you get a raise, a promotion or both.

This has never been more true than it is today. Think about it. The largest working block of employees are just now starting to retire enmasse. There will be a shortfall of competent workers and businesses will be competing more and more for that shrinking good talent pool.

What an opportunity for you!

what to do?

Do what you enjoy, to a point.

I know guys who are struggling in a band and trying to make it as professional golfers and hockey players. That is all wonderful. I affirm them in their desire to follow their dream and their passion.

But, when you have a family to support and obligations to attend to it is time to hang up the dream and start taking care of business. These men I know are in their late thirties and early forties.[13] With a wife and kids to support, it is time to do what must be done to take care of your family. Failure to do that is the equivalent of being on the backside of God.[19]

[19]By the way, the band "Mid Life Crisis" I spoke of earlier, all have "real jobs" too. They are bankers, doctors etc.
[14]But if anyone does not provide for his own, and especially for those of his household, he has denied the faith and is worse than an unbeliever. 1 Timothy 5:8

Don't be afraid to move around a bit either. Way back when, it was normal for a person to hire in to a company and stay there until retirement. From "cradle to grave" they said. The job market today however is vastly different.

Every three to four years, if you are not growing in your position, you may want to consider looking somewhere else.

What should you do on the job? Well, as Shakespeare said, "All the world is a stage."

You are always on. Walk the walk and talk the talk.

People are always watching too. You should think like a man on a donkey. The man is your mind and the donkey is your body. One is thought, the other action. One is spirit the other is flesh. People only can see your actions, but those actions are controlled by your thoughts and beliefs.

The problem occurs when I act completely inconsistent with my beliefs. Then there is the occasion where I think I am acting consistently only to find that I am not.

The best example of that is when I gave a great speech only to find that my zipper to my pants was open. Oops! Or the time when I had a great lunch meeting, only to excuse myself to the bathroom, there noticing a piece of food on my face. Yuck!

That is why feedback is so important. You must have people in your life that will tell you when you have the equivalent of ketchup on your face. You want to know as soon as possible so you can wipe it off!

If you have an irritating habit or rude manner (like chewing with you mouth open!) fix it! People judge how you look, how you act, what you do, what you say, what you wear . . . . .they are judging you **all the time**.

I spoke with one student who said that "people shouldn't judge, they should just look at the heart". Well, guess what? They do judge what they see, because they can't look into your heart. Don't waste your time trying to change the way things have always been, and will always be. Just work with it and swing the odds in your favor as best you can by looking, acting and doing your very best.

A good plan may be to work on the way you "look" for others, and take care of your "heart" for God. But, the reality is, when you look good on the outside, you feel better on the inside too. Likewise, if your heart is clean, it is a safe bet that you will be clean on the outside as well. They seem to go hand in hand.

Which comes first, heart or looks? Who cares? Work on them both. Just do what you can; and get the ball rolling!

Learn to Follow

It is a good bet that you will never be a good leader until you learn how to be a good follower. This is similar to my earlier observation that you will never get that which is your own until you help another get what they want.

Don't worry so much about being taken advantage of either. There is nothing more futile that than to try and worry about all the other people at work: whether or not they are playing the game fairly, getting ahead faster, pulling their weight, are they sharing and pulling to the tempo of the team.

There are two kinds of "people worry" as Mr. Boyington says:
1. Worry about everyone else.
2. Let everyone else worry about you.

It is simpler and much more beneficial (ie PROFITABLE) to hold your head high, play the game straight and take your chances.

Remember that the world does not owe you ANYTHING. A job is a privilege, and not a right. Yes, even a job at McDonalds flippin' burgers.

One of my kids asked me where they should get a job. Without hesitation I said "McDonalds of course." I could tell that she actually liked that answer (because she likes the fries, of course), but still wanted to know why.

What better place to learn a proven system, interact with coworkers, customers and management, to learn how to show up on time, put in a hard day's work and learn how to work as a team in the marketplace. Plus, hopefully, you will bring home some fries for dad from time to time!

This opportunity is available to all of those with a pleasant smile and willing work ethic. You have just started climbing the ladder in the marketplace. Stay there if you want, but after a few weeks, months, years there of proven dependability and value added, what company wouldn't want to hire you?

I'm Flippin' Burgers Man!

I recently stopped into a McDonalds and noticed a young man picking up a carpet and straightening up the place. He had a uniform on that led me to believe that he was in management. I asked him what he did there and he confirmed my belief. He was in fact the store manager.

He looked quite young so I asked him how old he was.

"Twenty-Three", he said.

He went on to say that he started working part-time at the McDonalds when he was 16 years old and worked his way up. Now he manages his own store, has health insurance, 401-k, performance bonuses and of course food discounts. All of this without a college education or any additional work experience.

Don't believe the lie told by the media that flipping burgers is a joke. They mock the very opportunity that helps many kids get ahead in life. Those fast food joints teach work skills and responsibility sorely needed today. Remember that a first job is a starting point. Stay there if you wish, but move on when your skills have outgrown the job.

Bob Boyington in his book, "You're Daddy Ain't Rich . . so you Have To Work" says that "there are really only four things that an employee brings to the employer. They are his mind, body, experience and reputation. As a new employee, all you have to offer is the first two: mind and body. The other two, combined with time are up to us."

"You must be honest and face facts when analyzing your true place and value as part of the workforce."

That, my friends, is where the rubber meets the road. You may be a valuable son or daughter, a valuable member of your football or gymnastics team, (obviously you have value to God), but, the marketplace is only interested in what you have of value to them. The marketplace always measures value in profit or gain.

Anything that you can do to increase your value will make you more valuable to the marketplace. One of the best things you can do to increase your value is to develop your mind. That was the message in the wisdom chapter and it is guaranteed to increase the value you bring to the marketplace by at least 50% (translated: learn how to get more for the same hour of time that you give to the marketplace.)

The "Duh's" of work:
1. Look as good as you can. *(see health chapter)*
2. Act as well as you can. *(see spirituality chapter)*
3. Learn as much as you can. *(see wisdom chapter)*
4. Earn as much as you can *(see wealth chapter)*

Do what you have to do so you can do what you want to do. Or as Dave Ramsey says, "Live like no one else will so you can live like no one else can."

A good thing to remember is to never complain about anything unless you have a solution. Without a solution or an idea to change things you are just wasting everybody's time.

Consistency is also very important at the workplace. It is good to always be helpful, caring and interested to help others do their functions at work. But, consistency is the real key. Coworkers deserve to know what kind of person we are and how we will probably act or react in any situation. This is true for all employees looking to get ahead, but especially true for those aspiring to or who are already in management.

Sources and other books to consider:

"Your Daddy Ain't Rich, So You Have To Work" by Bob Boyington
"Good to Great" by Jim Collins
"48 Days To The Work You Love" by Dan Miller
"E-Myth" by Michael Gerber

enjoy what you do

Consider this quote from the "Millionaire Next Door"

"There are more people (employees) today working at jobs they don't like. I'll tell you honestly that the successful man is a guy who works at a job, who likes his work, who can't wait to get up in the morning to get down to the office, and that's my criteria. And I've always been that way. I can't wait to get up and get down to the office and get my job under way."

It is funny that many of these quotes sound like they come out of the Bible. The following verse came from Ecclesiastes 5:18.

"Here is what I have seen to be good and fitting: to eat, to drink and enjoy oneself in all one's labor in which he toils under the sun during the few years of his life which God has given him; for this is his reward."

Calvin Coolidge said, "*Nothing in the world can take the place of persistence. Talent will not; nothing is more common than unsuccessful men with talent. Genius will not; unrewarded genius is almost a proverb. Education will not; the world is full of educated derelicts. Persistence and determination alone are omnipotent.*"

Without work, nothing gets done.

The next chapter will touch on the following:
- The single best investment idea to earn 20% per year.
- The secret that all wealthy people know.
- Why profit is such a good thing.

wealth

"Try not to become a man of success but rather to become a man of value."
-Albert Einstein

"Beloved, I pray that in all respects you may prosper and be in good health, just as your soul prospers."
-3 John 2

There seems to be a lot of fuzzy thinking with regard to wealth these days. It is at the core of the conflict many people have. Some see profit and wealth as evil, while others view profit and wealth as an increased responsibility to steward or manage their gifts.

The one thing for certain is that you cannot serve both money and God. But, I also think that the "fuzzy " thinking comes from not having a proper mindset with regard to both.

Wealth ultimately comes from God, but there is also the work and planning that you add to the equation. Going to work, earning as much as you can in the service of people, as opposed at the expense of people, is the wise thing to do.

An ancient text says that if you want to be great you must serve, and if you want to be first you must serve all.[20] Work is a perfect environment to put that teaching into action.

But, because there seems to be this conflict with regard to wealth, people have sold out their future to live a lifestyle beyond their means and have so much debt that they can't see straight.

Wealth is a practical and wise thing to put to use. But, remember, just like everything else you have in life, wealth will either be a tool or an idol. Money itself is not evil, but the love on money is. Use money and wealth, don't let it use you.

So, what are the half dozen keys to being wealthy?

Plan, earn as much as you can, frugality and spending, generosity, debt is bad, the habit of saving and, of course, get married.

You may be thinking to yourself, "That doesn't sound either difficult or exciting." You are right. It isn't. Millionaires are boring in fact. According to the book the Millionaire Next Door, 80% of all millionaires in the USA are first generation wealthy. That means that they did not inherit it: no trust funds, not sports stars or celebrities either.

Millionaires live on less than they make and live in modest neighborhoods compared to their wealth. They are well educated and married with three children. They also work between 45 and 55 hours per week.

Living in America can actually be a detriment to becoming wealthy. The longer a person lives in America the less likely he or she is to become a millionaire. Why is this the case? Because we are a "consumption based society." In general, the longer the average member of an ancestry group has been in America, the more likely he or she will become fully socialized to our high-consumption lifestyle.

---

[20]Mark 10:43-44 "But it is not this way among you, but whoever wishes to become great among you shall be your servant; and whoever wishes to be first among you shall be slave of all.

There is another reason. First-generation Americans tend to be self-employed. Self-employment is a major positive correlate to wealth. The "next-generation" is often less productive economically than the last.

There have been literally thousands of books, tapes and seminars designed and developed for getting rich quickly.

What I keep waiting for is the book that teaches one how to get rich slowly. In fact, the reason there isn't a good book about getting rich slowly is two-fold.

1. Nobody would be interested.

2. It takes too long.

That being said, this is the shortcut and the only true way. Here is the key to guaranteed riches in life. Get a job, spend less than you make and invest the rest. I guarantee that if you follow that plan, you will be wealthy. Piece of cake. Next subject.

In fact, the book reports that immigrants are four times more likely to become millionaires than if you were born in this country.

Millionaires are hardly what you would expect. In fact, they are frugal beyond belief. Many you will not even notice in a room or a shopping mall.

One millionaire when asked if he would like a glass of 1970 Bordeaux (a very expensive red wine) responded by saying, "I drink scotch and two kinds of beer – free and Budweiser."

People that do not have a lot of money don't seem to realize that millionaires are under a constant barrage from people who try and separate them from their money. Millionaires try to stay under the radar as much as possible. It is not uncommon for them to be found in blue jeans and a sweatshirt because they do not want to draw attention to themselves.

There are the aberrations of course: the ostentatious and flashy. These are atypical and more often than not do not have the net worth of their quiet and discrete contemporaries.

89

foundations for wealth

1. Earn as much as you can, spend less than you make and invest the rest.

Education plays a huge role in the earning power, but more often than not the higher the income the higher the expenses that go along with it. Income alone is not a determining factor in wealth. Rather the plan is.

I used to play this game with my kids called Cash Flow 101 by Robert T. Kiyosaki. It is a good game to help teach some basic principles about life and wealth.

In the game we each draw a card at random that determines our job and income. Some draw a school teacher and others draw a pilot or an attorney or a doctor. The income and expense ratio is very consistent. The higher the income the higher the expenses.

What determines the winner is the rate at which you can get your "passive income" (that is your investments and the dividends or interest they pay) to exceed your expenses.

You can see that the higher the expense, the larger the investments need to be. Smaller expenses, smaller investment required.

So, what makes the rich rich is their ability to be frugal (keep expenses low) and save as much as possible (increase their investments).

"Beware of little expenses, a small leak can sink a great ship."
-Benjamin Franklin

2. Great investment idea #2 **Start saving early then stop (if you want to).**

That's right, start early, then stop. When I used to work as an investment counselor I would use the following example. I would ask people to answer the following question:

"Who will have more money when they retire; The person who starts to invest $40 each week at age 25 and then stops at age 31, or the person who waits until age 31 and then continues to invest the same $40 for the rest of their lives?

Answer: The person who started early and then stops. Obviously, if the person continues to invest the $40 for the rest of their lives they will have much more, but the point is the importance of time on your money. "Timing" the market isn't nearly as important as "time in" the market. Why? Because of the greatest invention ever created (according to Albert Einstein), compound interest.

It looks something like this:

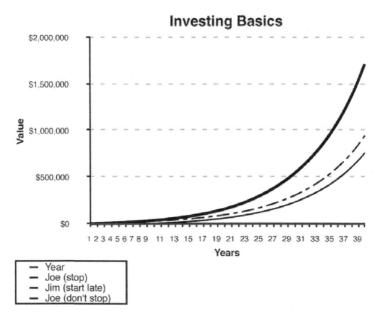

The bottom line is that by waiting six years to start the investment program you will forfeit almost $200,000 in wealth. If you are already over 25 the math still works out the same. You will be better off by starting now than by waiting to start later.

But, if you are under 25 you have a huge advantage! Remember, we are not talking big bucks either. Only $40 each week, that's about $1 per hour that you work. Use the tax advantage accounts like a 401-k or IRA and you come out even better.

Now, if you are over 25 don't get discouraged. The same will hold true if you are 30 and don't start until you are 37. The point is, where ever you are, just do it and get started.

You talk with any wealthy person and they almost always have a story about how they failed over and over again before they were successful.

Rich DeVos, one of the founders of the Amway corporation tells of his earlier bankruptcies before he made it big. His business acumen and wisdom provide opportunities (serving people) for individuals and families to have their own businesses.

Walt Disney lost everything as a cartoonist exploring his original ideas and would never have made it without the help of his brother Roy.

What Walt had was a creative genius and wisdom that he reinvested into his dream of creating (serving families) through an amusement park where families could have fun together.

These "success" stories were based on wisdom. They each lost all of their money more than once. But, nobody could take away their wisdom and desire to serve people.

Invest heavily in your wisdom and education for it is something that can never be taken away and can always be "sold" in the market place at the service of other people.

keep it simple

"Where should I put my money?" is a common question for the new investor. As a general rule the younger you are the more risk you can take (ie stocks and mutual funds), as you get older the less risk you can afford to take.

(In terms of sophistication), I love the comment from financial economist and Nobel laureate Harry Markowitz. He is one of the founders of modern portfolio theory. When asked about how to invest his money between risky and less risky investments he said,

" *I should have computed the historic covariance of the asset classes and drawn an efficient frontier. Instead. . . . I split my contributions fifty-fifty between stocks (riskier) and bonds (less risky)."*
Quoted in Zweig 1998

Want a simple rule of thumb? Invest your age in safe assets like bonds, savings and CD's and invest the balance in stocks and stock mutual funds. If you are 20 put 20% in safety and 80% in stocks. If you are 50, put 50% in safety etc.

There are lots of investment "gurus" out there, but my personal favorite is Dave Ramsey. Start with his Total Money Makeover and grow from there. Just keep it simple. Spend less than you make and invest the rest.

I live in a city where there is a huge house that was built years ago. My daughter asked me about it and I told her that it was the Gerber Baby Food mansion. She didn't think that it was right that someone has a house that big when so many people are hungry and cold.

She has a good point and a great heart. So, I asked her. If this guy provided a great service to families all over the world by creating and distributing a good food to babies shouldn't he get rewarded in the marketplace for providing that service?

On top of that, what if his job was able to provide thousands of great jobs to other families?

Plus, the larger and more profitable the company, the more in taxes that are being paid to the cities and states in which that company has factories.

Now, tell me, based on all of the people he is serving; why shouldn't he have such a large house? What we have set up in this county is if you want to become great and to be first among many, you must serve the most.

Remember that old ancient wisdom from earlier in the chapter? Those who want to be great among you shall be your servant, and whoever wants to be first among you shall be slave of them all.

A slave is a servant. So, to the degree that you serve more and more people, you will become great.

The question is, how are you serving others? How valuable is your service? I you don't make very much it's because the marketplace does not see what you are doing as very valuable.

So, increase your value to the marketplace by serving them better. The market will respond to you meeting a need, either perceived or real.

profit is good

By hindering the profit motive we are destroying the very basis for effort and achievement . Remember, they tried to do that in a country called the Soviet Union. They thought it best to be altruistic and work for the common good. You know what it did? It destroyed everything that it touched. It never left a profit; it only took and destroyed. It killed people by annihilating hope and profit and then literally killed people, millions of them in fact. Everyone was the same, the only thing that mattered was the government. If you didn't think so, you died.

That country, by the way, collapsed. It was a huge failure. Big government and altruism always are.

Did you know that the first settlers that came to America had the same idea as the Soviet Union? The earlier settlers came to this country primarily to avoid religious persecution from Europe and to advance the spread of Christianity.

Before the crew from the Mayflower left the boat they were determined to set up a civil form of government that would provide for all. It was called the Mayflower Compact. It used to be taught in public schools across the country until about 20 years ago. Too many references to God in it, I guess, so they stopped.

Anyway, they had an altruistic program where "all for one and one for all" was their motto. The first two years they were almost completely destroyed. Why? When people can get the same return with a small amount of effort as with a large amount, people will make little effort. Theft, laziness and corruption were so pronounced that they had to find a better way.

One of the elders pulled a quote from the Bible that said, "He who does not provide for his family is worse than an infidel"[21] and "Do not merely look out for your interest, but also the interest of others"[22] It was from these verses

[21] 1Timothy 5:8* But if anyone does not provide for his own, and especially for those of his household, he has denied the faith and is worse than an unbeliever.
[22] Philippians 2:4 5:8

that the leaders divided up the land and assigned all of the widows and orphans to individual families and said in essence, "Take care of those in your own family first." Socialism gave way to private farming and the results were dramatic.[23]

Taking care of the individual first not only solved the problem of lack and need, it also created wealth and prosperity for others as well. It was the profit motive that turned things around. A wise person understands that we are all motivated by hope and gain and profit. Hope is a future benefit. It is how we are all wired.

what you know affects your investment power

The best investment is paid off debt.

Here is an investment idea that will provide you with a guaranteed tax free 14% return on your money. Impossible you say? Far from it. Most people carry at least $9900 in credit card debt with an annual percentage of at least 14%. So, paying it off is like giving yourself a 14% after tax return on your money.

credit is bad, debt is bad, cash is king.

Buying on credit inflates the cost of things. A purchase with plastic or credit increases the price paid by an average of 20%.

I love the survival of the fittest shows where a lion is stalking the gazelle. We waits. He's patient. The gazelle moves in closer, oblivious to what is about to happen. Then all of a sudden the lion is on him like a spring on a trap.

In terror and panic the gazelle bolts like a prisoner breaking from jail. But, it's too late. The lion latches on and overcomes the gazelle.

Many Americans feel that way every day. They get up to go to work because of the lion. He is right there ready to pounce if you do not make the payment. The worker is not free, he works for the debt company and the bank.

---

[23]John Stosser article "The Tragedy of the Commons" Nov 21, 2007

Pay that sucker off, and you will be free indeed. Have the same fear of debt that the gazelle has of the lion. No, debt is not your friend. Thinking otherwise is naïve and you will pay a heavy price for that error in thinking.

How do I know? I have lived the lie and know it all to well.

Dave Ramsey does the best job teaching about this is. He is funny, smart and has practical "baby steps" to help you get out and stay of out the jaws of the lion. Website www.daveramsey.com

The world is shouting:
"Show me the money!" -Jerry Maguire *"Greed is good."* -Wall Street

One of the most potent addictions, financially speaking, is the mixing of
debt, greed and luxury. Greed fueling the desire for luxury funded by debt is
what crack cocaine does to the junkie on the street. Temporary exhilaration
leaving a path of destruction and despair.

Remember, profit is not the same thing as greed. Greed is bad. Profit
however is healthy and good. Greed is at the expense of someone, profit is in
service to someone. I teach my kids that you earn a profit when you leave
something better than you found it. A manufacturer takes raw materials and
works them, molds them and assembles them into a product that people are
willing to pay more than it cost to build. That is a good thing.

Then, with those profits the business can try and create other products
and earn more profit. Extra money gets invested into stocks (other companies) or banks (other companies and individuals) where it can be utilized by
other profit minded individuals.

The perception today is that profit is somehow evil and that it was created by taking advantage of somebody. Of course that happens, look at Enron
and the $850 BILLION mortgage bailout. But, the overwhelming majority
of businesses and business owners are good ethical people who follow the
rules. They are the ones creating the jobs and providing the products and
services that others want and need. In other words, they are doing a great
job of serving other people.

If they cease to have a profit motive, or the profit motive is stripped from
them through excess taxes and red tape, businesses will move out of this
country or cease to exist all together, thereby no longer serving people. I see
this first hand in Michigan. We are in a one state recession due to that faulty
philosophy.

Profit is a very good thing. You can do infinitely more with profit than
you can with loss. It is the only wise way to live; for businesses and for families as well.